IC assign NI
Quality NI
1-15-99
20.00

CUBANS

CUBANS

THE ULTIMATE CIGARS

WILLIAM P. MARA

The Lyons Press

Printed in the United States of America
Design and composition by Rohani Design, Edmonds, WA

10 9 8 7 6 5 4 3 2 1

Library of Congress Cataloging-in-Publication Data
Mara, W. P.
    Cubans: the ultimate cigars / William P. Mara.
      p. cm.
    Includes bibliographical references and index.
    ISBN 1-55821-644-8 (cloth)
    1. Cigar industry—Cuba. 2. Cigars. I. Title.
HD9149.C5C845   1998
338.4'767972'097291—dc21   98-16877
                            CIP

To Tracey, my wife and closest friend,

who tolerates the smoke with a quiet grumble

and nothing more.

Contents

Acknowledgments

SO MANY PEOPLE GAVE LAVISHLY OF themselves to make this book come to life, and to all of them I will always be grateful:

To Herbert Axelrod and Bernie Duke, who guided me around the many dangers that face any American traveling in Cuba; to the fine people at the Office of Foreign Assets Control, who were decent and understanding enough to let me do what was required to make this book worthwhile; to Bob Ramos, Michael Goldner, Frank Winters, and Jose Suarez of Havana Cigars in Union City, New Jersey, who treated a stranger like a friend and continue to make some of the finest non-Cuban cigars in the world; to all the friends I left behind in Cuba, not to mention those in America who are of Cuban origin, who imparted valuable advice and information regardless of any fears that may have counseled otherwise; to Erika and Peter Weiss-Geissler, my dear friends on the other side of the world; to Todd and company at Sure Photo in Neptune, New Jersey, the only people I would ever trust with such priceless fare; to Nick Lyons, Peter Burford, and Christina Rudofsky, my publishers, who uncomplainingly gave me whatever I needed (including an extended deadline) and never lost faith; to Chris Pavone, my editor and my friend, who is now stuck with more Cuban-cigar knowledge than he probably ever wanted; and last but far from least, to all my other friends who share my love for fine "smokables"—Jim Luchansky, Bob Quick, Scott Evans, Doug and Andy Hall, Aaron Salkin, Mickey Guerriero, Walt Zera, Steve Schummer, Deb "Debba" Mulkewycz, and DeeAnne Glenn. I want you guys to know you were the *real* motivation behind this project. It's about time I wrote something you might actually want to read.

Introduction

IF YOU'VE BOUGHT THIS BOOK, CHANCES are you consider yourself something of a connoisseur of fine cigars or would at least like to become one. If you are a resident of the United States and you were born after 1962, you've either never sampled a Cuban cigar or have done so under illegal circumstances. Those of you who live elsewhere are in the fortunate position of being able to simply visit your local smoke shop in order to partake the pleasure of such an experience. No matter which of these categories describes you, this book was designed to whet your appetite for the most famous and undoubtedly finest of all cigars: Cubans.

This is not a college-level textbook built under the presumption that you will use it to garner a doctorate on the subject. This book, like the cigars themselves, is intended to provide enjoyment and relaxation. It should be read during quiet hours, preferably in concert with either a cigar of Cuban origin or, if legalities don't permit that, one that is nearly comparable (of course none are seamlessly comparable, but a few are close).

I have tried to make the text as smooth and painless as possible. To that end I have consciously avoided the extensive use of Spanish terminology. During my research I was bombarded by such jargon in other publications (out of politeness I will not cite which) and always came away from them with the same conditions—a severe headache and watery, puffy eyes. I do not claim to be an expert in the Spanish language, melodic though it may be, and I will assume most of you are of similar mind. If you are indeed curious about the Spanish terms that refer to the world of Havana cigars, I've included a short vocabulary section toward the back, and I encourage you to indulge in any of the many other cigar-related publications that offer this terminology in such abundance. But again I point out that I purposely did not use these words because I wanted you to be able to easily absorb the *information* being transmitted, and not have to break the flow of digestion every few sentences to burn a new word and its meaning into your brain.

It is my most sincere wish that this book increases your appreciation not only for the cigars of Cuba but for cigars overall—especially after reading the section on cigar production and realizing just how much work goes into each one. In Cuba the creation of cigars has evolved over hundreds of years, and most cigar workers labor for long hours and in unpleasant conditions. Sappy though it may sound, each and every cigar made for export in Cuba is more than a simple luxury product; it is a work of art.

As a resident of the United States, born shortly after the embargo against Cuba was enacted, I have never been able to legally purchase Cuban cigars in my country. But it is one of my greatest wishes that one day the United States and Cuba will again be on friendly terms, and I am confident that this day will come long before I am gone, and I and many other American smokers will rejoice. I already have my celebratory plans carefully plotted: I will drive to a small shop that is owned by a friend and purchase either a Cohiba Esplendido or a Romeo y Julieta Churchill, regardless of cost. Then I will also buy him one, and we will smoke together and talk of all the good times ahead.

Until then many cigar lovers will have to content themselves only with information, which thankfully is free for the taking. Perhaps this book should be considered something of a preface to that glorious day.

History of
the Cuban Cigar
Industry

FROM THE EARLIEST TRACES OF ITS history, the tobacco of Cuba has been held in the highest regard, although sugar undoubtedly is Cuba's most important crop economically. As with any other form of history, facts often intermingle with fiction, and the shape of reality takes on a sharper edge only as the chronology moves closer to the present.

Most historians of the Cuban cigar start with Christopher Columbus's landing on Cuba's eastern shores in October 1492. But let's take a step back before even that and try to figure out how tobacco got to Cuba in the first place, about which there are only theories and very little in the way of solid evidence. The plant we know today as tobacco is scientifically classified in the genus *Nicotiana.* It has been suggested that the species *Nicotiana rustica* was growing in Cuba when Columbus and his men first arrived, but no examples of this particular variety are found there today. On the other hand, examples of *Nicotiana tabacum,* which is the species used in all modern Cuban-cigar manufacture, are known to have been growing in nearby South and Central America. It is therefore reasonable to believe that the seeds of this species were brought to Cuba by migrating Arawak Indians, the fore-runners of the Cuban Taino Indians. Although the Cuban climate was slightly different from that of South America, the Arawak's homeland, the alien form of tobacco simply learned to adapt, as many introduced organisms do, to its new environment.

6

Enter the Spanish explorer Christopher Columbus, who landed on Cuba's eastern shores in mid-October 1492, and claimed Cuba as the property of Spain. He later wrote that he thought the island was one of the most beautiful places he had ever seen, and he named it San Salvador. A few weeks later he sailed westward and landed again, this time in modern-day Bahía de Gibara. On November 2 he sent two of his men—Luis de Torres and Rodrigo de Xeres—inland, hoping to find the golden cities of the Great Khan. Torres and Xeres returned some four days later with no reports of Khan. They did, however, discover something else: natives carrying around long tubes made of leaves and stuffed with more leaves, which they sucked from one end while the other end burned.

The agrarian Tainos had learned to cultivate and cure the leaves of the tobacco plants, and soon they had begun rolling them into crude cigar shapes, bunching the leaves together and then wrapping them into another leaf. The Tainos would light one end and inhale deeply from the other. No doubt these earliest Cubans either developed very resilient lungs or just died quite young. How or why they came up with the notion of rolling and smoking tobacco in the first place has never been clear, so the true origin of the cigar may never be known. Columbus, notably, did not make a great fanfare at this discovery of what was to become one of the most infamous leisure products the world has ever known. It is believed that he did not develop a fondness for smoking and therefore was unsure of what to do with the gift of tobacco leaves given to him by the natives.

Future colonists, on the other hand, had no problem figuring out what to do with tobacco. By the early sixteenth century, not long after Diego Velázquez founded the cities Trinidad and Sancti Spíritus, Spanish settlers had learned from the Tainos how to cultivate and prepare tobacco. It found its way back to the Old World via cargo ships and other travelers, many of whom found tobacco most appealing and were more than happy to broadcast their joy when they arrived home. Toward the end of the middle of the century, Cuban tobacco was all the rage in both Europe and the Far East. By the early seventeenth century, production had been expanded not only in Cuba but also to Santo Domingo, Brazil, and in some of the new colonies on the eastern shores of what would one day become the United States. Demand ran high from nearly every major nation in the Old World, including Belgium, Germany, Holland, and even Japan and China. Spain had indeed discovered a valuable little sector of the world, and as its value increased, so did Spain's determination to control it.

One of the most common early uses of Cuban tobacco was as a form of medication. In 1635 a law was passed in (then) Persia forbidding its sale by anyone other than a licensed druggist, and as late as

8

the early twentieth century many people swore that tobacco's greatest value was to physicians and pharmacists: It supposedly could be used in one form or another to treat everything from colic and bone fractures to tetanus. It was an ingredient in lotions, ointments, powders, and pills. Even the application of moistened tobacco leaves was said to have miraculous healing powers, applicable to everything from hemorrhoids to severe burns. Probably the most prominent figure in this aspect of tobacco's history is Jean Nicot, the French ambassador to Lisbon, who was part of the consensus that tobacco had great medicinal qualities. His name was forever linked with the plant when it was Latinized to form tobacco's genus name, *Nicotiana.*

9

Whatever tobacco's uses, the demand for it skyrocketed in the sixteenth century, and by the early seventeenth century the Cuban tobacco industry began to organize itself. Previously there had been virtually no rules or laws by which production was governed. Naturally, in the absence of a restrictive bureaucracy, tobacco producers enjoyed a measure of prosperity and happiness. They were a self-governing body for the most part, with the colonial Spanish powers safely tucked away on the other side of the ocean.

But then Spain stepped in and began laying down parameters. In 1614 the king of Spain ordered all tobacco meant for international sale to be first registered in Seville, which was then considered the tobacco capital of the world. This was the first step toward what would eventually become total Spanish control.

Back in Cuba one problem that had arisen was the use of nearly every parcel of arable land for growing the lucrative tobacco and sugar crops. Farmers fought for space, and some simply grew their tobacco in areas that didn't belong to them. There were shortages of fruits and vegetables, and rich forested areas were being cut down to make room for more tobacco plantations.

Cuba worked its way through these annoyances and continued to supply the world with its now-famous product. There was a great deal of money being channeled into the Cuban tobacco industry, which was one of the primary sources of income for the island. The powers-that-were in Spain took notice of this and decided they wanted an even bigger piece of the pie. In 1717 they enacted a monopoly on all Cuban tobacco, driven largely by their desire to replenish their nation's funds after the War of the Spanish Succession

(1701–14). The monopoly was designed and imposed by the king and was regulated by the sovereign powers that had already been installed on the island. In simple terms, the monopoly forbade tobacco growers from selling their wares to anyone except Spain. Like nearly all monopolies inspired by greed and the insatiable hunger for control, this enaction sparked off nothing but trouble.

All tobacco grown in Cuba was to be sent straight to Seville, where it would then be distributed to buyers under the supervision of Spanish officials. The temptation for blatant avarice proved overwhelming for the Spanish government, which didn't waste any time taking a huge portion of the profits and giving the Cubans little more than a pittance for their sweat and toil. The farmers vigorously rebelled, and violent confrontations ensued. (Ironically, some of the farmers tried to avoid conflict by moving west, which placed them in the center of what they would soon discover to be a tobacco grower's paradise—the Vuelta Abajo.)

The monopoly was lifted in 1723 after nearly six years of continuous farmers' revolts, but it was reenacted in 1761, once the colonial powers were convinced that things had calmed down. It didn't last long this time either: In 1762 the British occupied and took control of Cuba during the Seven Years' War (1756–63), and with it all the island's tobacco, sugar, and other crops. But their reign of power also didn't last long: They were driven out a year later, and again control of the Cuban tobacco industry ended up in Spain's hands. By 1764 the monopoly was back in place, but this time the farmers diplomatically submitted to it without much more than the occasional grumble, at least on the outside. On the inside, however, rage and hatred were simmering.

Some positive developments did occur during this time. For one, the Spanish government, eager to supply the rest of the world with only the finest Cuban tobacco (and thereby to ensure continued high profits), established the first official grading and rating system: Leaves were separated into basic categories of color, texture, and quality. Then in 1789 the first true manual on properly growing tobacco was published by the Spanish monopoly's officiating body, and the rolling of cigars became more crisply defined, with the filler, binder, and wrapper leaves being acknowledged as separate and individual entities for the first time. And although small, privately owned rolling shops had long existed, in 1799 the first major, large-scale factory was opened. In a sense this signaled the beginning of true commercialization of the Cuban tobacco industry, which was no longer an innocent small-town operation. It was big business.

In June 1817 a breath of fresh air swept across the dispirited tobacco farmers: The Spanish monopoly was removed. Spain had a new leader, King Ferdinand, who was sensitive to the social changes going on in Europe and the rest of the world. He apparently felt the monopoly was becoming outdated and would soon collapse from the weight of its inherent dysfunctions. After much consideration he decided to dismantle his country's absolute control over Cuba's tobacco. At first the Cuban farmers were overjoyed, but then they discovered there was a string attached: a brutal taxation rate would continue to be paid to Spain, a "royal tribute" as they called it. The motherland would take as much as 20 percent of the island's entire tobacco yield.

Again the farmers took action, and this time they had built up enough of their own power to ensure that the final struggle for freedom would be a short one. They had become a wiser, more experienced legion, aware of what kind of resistance they could expect, and had grown in number. They were also sensitive to the fact that tobacco production depended wholly on their labor and talents. In short, they had grown formidable, and the old powers no longer had the luxury of oppressing them with minimal risk. Furthermore, by January 1827, after years of struggle, virtually all forms of Spanish tobacco taxation had been eliminated. The time for the industry to take its next evolutionary step had arrived.

For much of the remainder of the nineteenth century, the Cuban cigar industry bloomed. Hundreds of new brands appeared, including many of the still-surviving legends—Partagas, Por Larrañaga, La Corona, Punch, H. Upmann, and others. Foreign investors came in droves, setting up new shops and factories and buying what little farmland was still available. Gustave Bock started putting the first rings on cigars sometime in the 1830s (previously they had no such identification and were, in a word, "naked"), and Ramón Allones began offering the first cigars in boxes around 1845, replacing the cruder method of securing bundles by tying ribbons around them. Everyone else was following suit with both procedures by the 1880s.

During the 1850s the Cuban cigar industry rolled more than a half billion cigars, had more than fifteen hundred factories, and employed more than fifteen thousand workers. Many new communities arose around the newer farming regions directly as a result of the constant demand for more leaves, and life was relatively good for the workers. During this time Havana claimed its crown as the capital of the cigar industry.

Naturally, there were a few low points. One of the harshest occurred in 1856, when many factories began laying off employees and cutting off contracts with farmers because of the rumor that the United States—one of Cuba's key markets, consuming more than three hundred million cigars in 1855 alone—was getting ready to impose a stiff tariff on Cuban-imported tobacco. The rumors became reality on March 3, 1857, when Congress approved the tariff, and the Cuban tobacco business spiraled into a frenzy. Another hike in the duties was implemented in 1883. The United States was already making plenty of their own cigars and wanted to discourage further competition from Cuba.

Shortly after the Ten Years' War, during which Cuba tried unsuccessfully to free itself from Spanish rule, Spain raised the duty on many items imported from the United States in order to recoup some of the expenses lost during the conflict. As a result, America's exports to Spanish-ruled Cuba dropped considerably. In response, William McKinley, Ohio senator and future president, drew up what would become known as the McKinley Bill: It made an already tight avenue of opportunity for the Cuban tobacco industry even tighter, raising the import duties by more than 75 percent. Sugar profits were also affected.

By this time the American market was still taking around 120 million cigars from Cuba each year. Without that substantial outlet, Cuba had to either find other markets that would absorb the excess or begin cutting back production. The leaders of the Cuban tobacco industry, with few options from which to choose, were forced to ask Spain for help. Spain in turn outlined an agreement to purchase more Cuban tobacco, but again under the conditions of more control and more of the profits.

In view of the growing instability of the industry, many manufacturers began to form trusts and buy up brand names to ensure themselves a little security for what seemed to be rough times ahead. The trusts were conglomerations of large manufacturers who sort of "huddled together" to more effectively brace themselves against any forthcoming blows. They also, not coincidentally, crystallized into a formidable threat to the very existence of the smaller, independently owned firms.

Now Cubans were more determined than ever to gain their independence from Spain. Another uprising occurred in 1895, sparked off at least in part by the painful economic depression. In America, sensationalized reports of the harsh living conditions and of sovereign Spain's continuing insensitivity were being fed into the public mind, a crusade led largely by William Randolph Hearst and Joseph Pulitzer. This "yellow journalism," as it was to become known, stirred up a great deal of sympathy for the Cuban people, not to mention plenty of animosity toward Spain.

17

Spain tried its best to squash the revolt, but Cuba had become too powerful, not to mention too angry. Many Americans shared the sentiment that the United States should aggressively help the Cuban people in their quest for freedom, but President McKinley remained neutral. He did acknowledge, however, that many Americans visiting Cuba could be in danger, so he sent the battleship *Maine* into Havana Harbor on January 25, 1898, to monitor American safety. Less than a month later, on February 15, the *Maine* exploded, killing 260 people.

Naturally, Spain was blamed for the incident. Spain in turn denied having had any part in the disaster, suggesting that mechanical malfunction was the cause. A naval court of inquiry eventually decided that a submarine mine was the catalyst. By March President McKinley was demanding that Spain give Cuba its total and complete independence. Spain refused, and on April 25 the United States Congress declared that America and Spain were at war.

The Spanish-American War lasted only until the following August and resulted in relatively few American casualties. In December the Treaty of Paris was signed, and with it Spain at last released its grip on Cuba. America also extracted colonial power over Guam, Puerto Rico, and the Philippines. Notably, many Americans also wanted to acquire Cuba, but the nation had already suffered enough. It was time for them to start governing themselves and leave behind the toils and troubles that went hand-in-hand with being a colony.

Perhaps ironically, through the Platt Amendment—drawn up along with Cuba's first constitution in 1901—America was given a tract of land in the city of Guantánamo, around Guantánamo Bay, and quickly erected a naval base, which remains fully active to this day. (It has always been a source of great irritation to Fidel Castro, but the lease drawn up at the time specifically states that the United States does not have to vacate the area unless such action is agreed upon by both nations.)

With the turn of the century came a renewed period of prosperity for the Cuban cigar industry. Demand grew again in the United States and elsewhere, and Cuba had little trouble keeping up. In the new free and open market there were hundreds of registered cigar brands scattered among both independent companies and their rivals, the huge trusts. While the trusts were confident that their products would corner the bulk of sales, independents hedged their bets on the loyalty of consumers to specific blends and brand names. In the end both sides turned out fairly happy, for the huge trusts never cornered the market as they had hoped. In fact, the independents satisfied nearly a full half of the demand.

In the mid-1920s the Cuban cigar industry took its first shot at mechanization. American cigar manufacturers had already been using machines for a while. The response from the Cuban workers was quick and predictable: They wanted the government to ban cigar-making machines altogether. They cited the potential drop in quality, and then of reputation, of their world-famous habanos, and the obvious fact that many of the workers would end up unemployed. Furthermore the question of economics crept up: Were the machines even worth using in the first place? They would require frequent maintenance and could be run only by specially trained personnel. They also couldn't produce many of the more unusual cigar shapes—figurados and torpedos, for example. A few factories employed machines anyway, and the government ordered them to inform the consumer that their cigars were machine-made by mentioning it on the outside of the packaging. By the end of the thirties, however, the industry was back to making everything by hand. The first thrust into the mechanized age had come to an end.

The stock-market crash of 1929 and the Great Depression that ensued had a devastating effect on the Cuban cigar industry. The United States wasn't the only nation affected by this dark period of financial collapse, and because so many of the world's markets were in a state of chaos, Cuban cigar manufacturers found it harder and harder to sell their products. They had many strikes against them. First there was the naturally high price of habanos: The last thing on a lot of people's minds during the thirties was spending money on a luxury item—some people didn't even have money for food, let alone cigars. Then there were the high export tariffs, which took another huge bite out of the manufacturers' profits. Cuban workers were making decent or at least respectable wages up to this point, and the industry leaders knew something had to give in that area as well. Suddenly mechanization seemed like a better idea than ever.

The workers naturally wanted nothing to do with wage cuts or cigar-making machines. Even if they had fallen in love with the idea, the other detriments—the high retail prices and brutal duty fees—would still have made survival of the industry difficult. To worsen matters, many foreign investors fled Cuba and took their money with them.

The strategy that was eventually adopted was to continue growing tobacco in Cuba (that of course could not change because a habano wouldn't be a habano without genuine Cuban leaves), then send it to the United States to be rolled, packaged, and so on. Smaller factories were also set up in towns not as "cigar-oriented" as Havana, and employees who were willing to work for low wages were hired. But still a goodly portion of the production was done in the United States, much of it in Trenton, New Jersey. This strategy worked out well for the Cuban cigar industry overall because the tariffs on raw materials exported to the United States were considerably lower than those imposed on finished products. And the American factories had no qualms about using machines, so production was much more efficient.

The beginning of the forties brought new promise to the Cuban industry, mainly because of the advent of World War II. One of the greatest advantages was America's involvement, which took workers out of the American factories and thus transferred much of the workload back to Cuba. Business in Cuba flourished again, but even the most casual observers of world trends knew that once the war was over production would dip again. It did exactly that, evident after the war when America once again took up its rolling, packaging, and distributing operations while relying on Cuba for raw materials only.

The fifties, unsurprisingly, started out sluggish for the Cuban industry. Many nations were too busy licking their wounds from the fighting to be concerned with bulk cigar purchases; England, for example, had been a huge market for Cuban cigars until it entered the conflict in 1939. Their nation was torn to shreds by the war, and they simply were in no condition economically to engage in many international dealings.

22

But by the mid-1950s business began to rise again, due to many factors. For one, the brains of the Cuban industry began searching for new markets and even attempted to reestablish old ones. They vigorously advertised their products and made many opening deals that, while small, still established new markets that would lead to much larger and more lucrative outlets in the years ahead. Rolling machines were finally utilized on a broad basis, and they were used for nearly all the cigars intended for international distribution. Many of the workers were disgusted by this, of course, but there is little doubt that the high productivity of the machines contributed to the survival of the industry during these threatening times. Another factor was the reduction of the United States' and Canada's duties, something both nations had been regularly promising for the prior two decades. And when Cuba began to develop a reputation as a tourist hot spot, the economy really began to percolate: Millions of travelers flocked to the beautiful Caribbean island, and with them came the currency that would be spent on, among other things, cigars.

— ～ —

Fidel Castro, born in the Oriente Province in 1927, was raised in a wealthy home but grew to despise people who supported a class system based on finance and affluence. He attended the University of Havana and graduated with a law degree in 1950. A short three years later, he made his first attempt to overtake the regime of then-president Fulgencio Batista, who was the very antithesis of Castro: wealthy, powerful, and a devoted capitalist. Batista had no problem allowing himself and his government to act as puppets for other, more powerful nations, the United States included. He was a true dictator who hoarded his nation's earnings while many Cubans went without food or shelter. Castro, who considered himself a champion of the poor and oppressed and claimed he subscribed to the belief that all people were equal, openly loathed Batista.

Much of Castro's anger was completely rational. Batista undoubtedly made a point of catering only to the richest and most powerful individuals. He ran Cuba, Havana in particular, with a near Mafia-like ruthlessness, gleefully accepting graft from a startling number of sources. He even rigged his own elections, which he knew was absolutely essential to retaining his grip on the nation. The lower classes and even most of the people in the middle class deeply resented the man and wanted him removed. But none had the means to do so. Fidel Castro, however, was determined to find a way.

Castro's first attempt to spark a revolution came on July 26, 1953, with an attack on the Moncada army barracks in Santiago de Cuba. The attack was poorly planned, and the majority of Castro's forces were either killed or captured; Castro himself was sent immediately to prison to serve a fifteen-year sentence. But Batista released him in 1955, mostly to quell public outcry and to avoid the development of too much sympathy toward Castro's crusade. Castro had chosen the perfect time to start a revolution, and he knew it: There were so many Cubans who wanted desperately to rid themselves of their current leader that Castro, imprisoned or not, had a very good chance of gaining support from the populace. This would eventually become his greatest asset, for both Batista and his friends in the United States severely underestimated his abilities. In a very real sense Castro made sure his army consisted not only of the rebels who stood alongside him in the heat of battle, but also of every other person in Cuba who wanted to topple Batista's government. And that was a large and powerful army indeed.

To memorialize the disaster of the failed attack, Castro began what he called the 26th of July Movement, which glorified those who died during the brief battle. Castro fled to Mexico City after his release from prison and prepared a new band of rebel forces for a second attack. He had learned a great deal from his initial defeat and made sure his next strike, which occurred in early December 1956, would be more powerful and considerably more organized. This time he chose Oriente as his theater, but again his forces, which consisted of around eighty soldiers, were soundly defeated. However, Castro and a handful of survivors escaped capture and fled into the Sierra Maestra Mountains. One of those survivors was Ernesto "Che" Guevara, a former Argentinean physician who had come into Castro's trust and friendship because the two men shared nearly identical political philosophies.

For the next two years Castro and his remaining followers waged nearly ceaseless guerrilla warfare. Batista tried desperately to eradicate the pest that Castro had become, but this time he had no success. At the same time, the animosity toward Batista among the ordinary citizens rose to the boiling point. Castro was being thought of as a cult hero, a romantic underdog fighting for the good of the people. Batista's hold on the nation was finally beginning to crumble.

At the end of 1958 a violent civil war erupted, and Batista's military forces were unable to quell it. Castro, who by now had developed a flawless sense of strategic timing, rolled into Havana with a fleet of tanks, and on January 1, 1959, Fulgencio Batista hurried out of Cuba and headed for the Dominican Republic. His days as Cuba's president were over.

The people of Cuba were thrilled at the prospect of having Castro as their new leader. They had bought into his image as a believer in equality and his promises of a better, happier Cuba. But no sooner had Castro taken control than he replaced capitalism with communism, and embarked on a process of nationalization that engulfed every major industry, the cigar business notwithstanding. Thousands of workers lost their jobs or were transferred to different ones, and billions of dollars worth of property was taken from foreign investors. The Cuban cigar industry became state property, enraging thousands, including American businesspeople.

In April 1961, President John F. Kennedy sanctioned an attempt to exterminate Castro's new regime through what would become known as the Bay of Pigs Invasion by forces that consisted primarily of Cuban exiles, led by the CIA. They were hastily trained, and a strategy was quickly and sloppily mapped out; Castro's army had little trouble defeating them. Naturally, America's relationship with Cuba then soured considerably.

The Cuban cigar industry was deeply affected: In early 1962 President John F. Kennedy imposed an economic embargo by the United States against Cuba, once again cutting off one of Cuba's largest cigar-buying markets, this time completely. The period of change that followed was one of the most radical in the cigar industry's history. It is somewhat amusing to note that Kennedy himself was a devoted smoker of Cuban cigars. A popular tale is that he asked one of his aides to gather up as many H. Upmann Petit Coronas, his personal favorite, that could be found in the Washington area the night before he signed the embargo.

28

After the embargo went into effect, relations between the United States and Cuba grew even worse. Russia also began setting up missile sites on the island in the summer of 1962. High-flying U.S. planes monitored this activity and returned with photographs that strongly suggested a military alliance between Castro and Russian Premier Nikita Khrushchev, a potential threat not only to the United States but also to any other nations in the Western Hemisphere that lay within striking distance. After a full week's private discussion and debate, President Kennedy announced to the American people the discovery of the missile sites, and declared a quarantine to halt the "delivery of offensive weapons and associated material to Cuba." The week that followed was perhaps the closest the world has ever come to nuclear war: American armed forces were at the highest levels of emergency alertness, prepared for anything. Kennedy announced that any attack on the United States by Cuba would also be considered an attack by the Soviet Union, requiring immediate retaliatory action; Khrushchev sent Kennedy impassioned letters, first demanding assurances that the United States would not invade Cuba, then demanding removal of American nuclear missiles from Turkey; an American U-2 reconnaissance plane was shot down over Cuba; and Soviet ships sailed toward the naval blockade. Finally, after these famous "Fourteen Days in October," Khrushchev announced that the construction of missile sites had been stopped, and the crisis slowly de-escalated.

In spite of the now-dead U.S. market, Cuba continued to supply Canada and Europe with both tobacco and sugar. In 1967 the well-known Swiss tobacco magnate Zino Davidoff offered to purchase Cuba's legendary El Laguito factory and manufacture the first cigars of the recently developed Cohiba brand. But the Cuban government declined, preferring to retain ownership of the Cohiba name. Davidoff instead produced the first cigars possessing the Cohiba blend under his own name. They became hugely successful, and in 1983 Cuban officials decided to market them on their own—and under the name Cohiba. This of course led to a conflict between Cuba and Davidoff that would push the latter to sever all business ties in 1988, taking his still-famous Davidoff line with him.

Today the Cuban cigar industry continues to produce their aromatic products primarily for the European market, most significantly Spain. Canada is also a steady consumer, as are a few smaller nations. The number of brands has shrunk to fewer than thirty-five, although it has been reported many times that Castro, who claims he no longer smokes cigars, continually encourages the industry to create new blends.

While there is little doubt that there will always be a place for Cuban cigars in the countries of the West, there also is little doubt that the Cuban cigar industry will flourish once again if a free-trade relationship reopened between Cuba and the United States. For the moment, however, this chapter in the history of Cuba's cigar industry has yet to be written.

Creation
of the
Cuban Cigar

TOBACCO HAS BEEN CULTIVATED IN Cuba for many hundreds of years. Most cigar enthusiasts know the story of Christopher Columbus landing on Cuba's shores and finding natives smoking crude versions of the cigars that have become so beloved today. The process of creating a fine habano has been passed down through many generations, during which it has undergone an evolution, gradually becoming more refined until it has reached a point of near perfection.

A question that has been asked many times by many people, some cigar smokers and some not, is: Are Cuban cigars really better than all others, and if so, why? The first answer can of course only be subjective, as there no doubt are cigar connoisseurs who prefer brands manufactured in other nations. It goes without saying, then, that the only opinion I can offer is my own. Having said this, I state for the record that, from my experiences, the best cigars Cuba has to offer are indeed the best in the world. Why? Quite simply because of their aroma. An easy-drawing, carefully rolled, and properly maintained Cohiba Esplendido or Romeo y Julieta Churchill cannot be matched by any other cigar in terms of flavor and bouquet. Habanos have, as I have said to many curious parties, the richest and fullest tobacco fragrance. They are the most *realized* cigars, and they set the standard for all others to follow—but never to fully duplicate. In a phrase, they are exactly what cigars are *supposed to be.*

THE TWO TYPES OF CUBAN CIGAR TOBACCO

Although all Cuban cigars are made from only one species of tobacco (*Nicotiana tabacum*), two different varieties are used: one intended for wrapper leaves, and the other intended for filler and binder leaves. Although the processes of growing, curing, fermenting, sorting, and rolling each is similar, they are not identical. Minor differences must be present simply by virtue of their different purposes.

PLANTING

The growing of all Cuban tobacco begins in the same way that it has for hundreds of years: with some seeds and a bit of soil. Cuba's soil is particularly renown, and rightly so. Since there is a variety of growing regions, there is also a variety of soils, each with their own pedological fingerprint: pH level, mineral content, and even color. The brick red soils of the Havana province, for example, are particularly famous, although not the norm throughout Cuba. Ideal tobacco-growing soil is loose and loamy, making it easy for the farmers to till, the water to penetrate, and the plants to root. Farmers also make a point of planting only in areas that are relatively flat, so all the nutrients will be evenly dispersed during rainstorms or watering sessions.

Evidence that soil is one of the keys to the high quality of Cuba's tobacco lies in the simple fact that cigars rolled from tobacco grown in other nations using "Cuban seed" (a distressingly popular marketing phrase) have never matched true habanos in flavor or redolence. (Along similar lines, some smokers will pay a premium for a cigar that has been hand-rolled by anyone who once lived in Cuba, as if that has anything to do with the flavor.) While the precise chemistry of Cuban soil may always remain a closely guarded secret, it would be nearly impossible to duplicate even if it wasn't. It also has been suggested that the salty sea air that envelops Cuba also contributes to the overall quality of the tobacco. But this same type of air can be found not only in other parts of Cuba aside from the prime tobacco-growing regions, but also in surrounding nations as well.

Tobacco seeds, which are about the size of the dot above this *i* and are distributed to the farmers by the government (which controls all of Cuba's tobacco industry), are usually planted in late September or early October. They begin their life in something called a nursery bed, where they germinate before being transplanted to a second bed. A young tobacco plant is very delicate, and the slightest aberration could easily destroy it, so the nursery bed must meet rigid standards: just the right amount of water, the right mineral composition, and so forth. There are professionals in Cuba whose job is to make sure these beds meet the prescribed standards. Nursery beds are carefully and caringly cultivated during the off-season so they will be in ideal condition come the fall.

36

The tobacco seeds are mixed with water in watering cans, and then a planter walks alongside the nursery rows and sprinkles the seed-water mixture. The seeds are scattered in a somewhat chaotic fashion, but since they will not be in these beds for long, neatness doesn't matter. It *is* important, however, for the planter not to lay out all the seeds in one day, but rather over the course of a few days, in the event that something—a pest infestation, for example—goes wrong.

GERMINATION

From the moment the seed is covered with soil, it requires constant attention, like a demanding invalid. Although delicate, tobacco is a voracious plant, draining a great deal of life out of its host and the people who care for it. The farmers must cover the nursery beds—commonly with cheesecloth, grass, or hay—so the young plants do not suffer the brutal effects of the Cuban sun or the beating of a sudden tropical downpour.

As the seed germinates (sprouts), the covering is removed a little at a time. By about the eighth or tenth day, all the covering has been removed, and the fields have changed from an earthy brown or red to a rich, healthy green. Not long after the uncovering, the sprouts are treated with a variety of pesticides and fungicides.

The Cuban climate naturally plays a large part in the development of all of Cuba's agricultural crops, but again it is not so unique that it could be considered a huge factor in the superior quality of Cuba's tobacco: Many nearby islands offer similar climate, as do parts of southern Florida, and yet the tobacco from those places has never matched that of Cuba's.

REPLANTING

Once the young plants reach a height of about 6 inches (15 centimeters), which usually takes a little more than a month, they are transplanted. This is a particularly tedious and backbreaking chore: The farmer must gently pull up each and every plant that appears healthy and get it to the maturing bed within a few hours, or it will die. Speed is of the utmost importance, and the farmers who perform this unenviable task must be quick and agile. Once the little plants have reached their destination, where they will spend the rest of their lives, they are chemically treated, primarily to fend off parasites.

As with the nursery beds, the soil of the maturing fields is carefully prepared long before

the young plants arrive. Again, trained professionals oversee this task and make adjustments
wherever necessary. (For the curious: Yes, Cuban
tobacco growers do indeed make use of whatever
man-made chemical concoctions are required to
ensure the highest quality of their crop.) The soil
of each region has its own set of characteristics,
thus ensuring the individual quality of each brand
of tobacco. It is a more formulated business than
one might imagine. So if the growing fields do not
live up to their own blueprint, changes must be
made until they do.

The plants are set into the maturing field one
by one, usually about 1 foot (.3 meters) apart. After
being replanted, the plant just sits there, droopy and
tired from the uprooting, looking as though it is only
days away from expiring. Occasionally a few plants
will indeed die off, and these will be discarded and
replaced. But usually they will quickly return to their
former glory. A field full of healthy tobacco plants,
so much like a legion of marching soldiers in their
neat and sturdy rows, is a proud sight to the farmers.
It is a monument to their labors and the promise of
greater achievements yet to come.

The job of raising the crop is far from over.
During the next few weeks, at carefully measured

intervals, the farmers perform myriad tasks, including irrigating, applying pesticides and fertilizers, checking for parasites, and adding soil to the base of the growing stalks to steady them. If the leaves are to be used for wrappers, then a cheesecloth roof is erected over the crop to weaken the effects of the sunlight; plants destined for binder and filler aren't given this kind of protection.

A grower must also be sure all the nutrients going into the plant find their way to the leaves rather than to competitive growths such as buds, suckers, and new shoots. As with all other aspects of tobacco cultivation, this is a time-consuming and highly detail-oriented responsibility. Each and every plant must be inspected almost daily, and offending buds or shoots must be removed immediately. Once a plant grows tall enough, it is tied to a stake so it continues to grow in the proper direction.

HARVEST

At full maturity the standard Cuban tobacco plant stands almost 6 feet (1.8 meters) high. It bears between sixteen and eighteen leaves arranged in six levels. In the case of plants bearing leaves to be used as wrappers, the leaves of each level have their own name, from top to bottom: *corona, centro gordo, centro fino, centro ligero, uno y medio,* and *libre de pie.* In the case of sun-grown (not protected under canopies) binder and filler leaves, only three names are used, from top to bottom: *ligero, seco,* and *volado.* With the binder and filler leaves, those of the *ligero* type are strongest because they have absorbed more sunlight than the others and therefore have become darker and more oily.

Wrapper leaves usually are harvested one level at a time (sometimes the entire plant is cut down, but not usually) starting at the bottom, because those leaves are the farthest along in development. The farmer allows about week to pass before clearing off the next level. The leaves usually are not cut but rather snapped gently with the fingers.

Binder and filler leaves are harvested much in the same way, but sometimes they may be taken from the top first rather than from the bottom; it all depends on how far along the farmer wants the leaves to develop. The harvester will cut right through the stem, taking two or three leaves at a time. These leaves may be used for binder and filler for cigars, but they also may eventually be ground into cigarette or pipe tobacco or sold on the international tobacco market.

The harvested leaves are collected in shallow trays or baskets (from one hundred to about three hundred at a time) and covered, then inspected for quality before being sent to the curing barn. Leaves that are judged unsuitable for cigar manufacture are not necessarily destroyed: They may end up in someone's pipe or within the roll of a cigarette.

CURING

The curing barns of Cuba are situated close to the growing fields, so the trip from picking to curing is a short one. The barns vary in style from traditional—some of which have been standing for decades—to modern. They usually feature a thatched roof and crudely made walls. The poles on which the leaves will hang are nothing more than relatively straight shafts of wood, often cut from whatever nearby tree offered a branch of qualifying dimensions. These poles are often relieved of their bark and then soaked in salt water for almost two months to remove any odors that would affect the natural scent of the slowly curing leaves. The more modern barns often have a corrugated steel roof and steel poles with convenient hooks or holes to hold the leaves' binding thread.

Each leaf is joined to another with the aid of a small needle and some cotton thread. The needle is flat, about 6 inches (15 centimeters) long, and shaped by a gentle curve. The leaves are joined in pairs, with the thread laced through the rib, just above the point where the leaf was snapped from the stalk.

A barn full of tobacco leaves is vaguely reminiscent of a slaughterhouse full of hanging meat. The rows are kept neat and orderly and are so dense that it is difficult to see what's behind them. The barns usually have very high ceilings, and they are always situated so their doors and windows will be in the path of the sun. The pairs of leaves are spaced evenly and closely, but not so closely that they are pressed together: Too-close contact may affect texture and overall flavor. Similarly, they are not allowed to touch the other poles that support the one on which they hang. Later they will be put in contact with one another intentionally and benefit from it. But not yet.

43

The climatic conditions in the barns are similar to those in a humidor. With humidors, the ideal numbers are 70 percent humidity and 70°F (21°C), and in the barns the figures are pretty much the same. Of course, there are many outside factors that will cause conditions to vary, so a constant watch must be kept. Depending on whether the temperature or humidity is too high or too low, the doors and windows are opened or closed;

sometimes heaters are installed to drive away excess moisture. The barn also does not have a uniformity of temperature and humidity in all of its own sectors: For example, the region closest to the ceiling is the warmest, since the heat from inside the barn rises and the heat of the blazing sun penetrates; so the bars that hold the rows of leaves are often moved vertically to ensure that all the leaves cure evenly.

It takes about a month and a half for the leaves to dry. During this time their color slowly changes, from a radiant green, to yellow, and then to the natural brown that most people identify with tobacco. It is during the latter stages of this process that the leaves begin to develop their pleasing and famous aroma. It is possible that part of the irresistible scent that is characteristic only of Cuban tobacco is developed because of the barns: So much tobacco has been cured here that the scent is sort of "passed on" to new leaves. One can't help but wonder if leaves grown and harvested in the Dominican Republic, Florida, or even Cameroon would improve in flavor if cured in a Cuban barn.

44

THE FIRST FERMENTATION

Once the curing process is over, the leaves are sorted by size and color. This is a much less intense sorting process than the ones that follow: Each cigar leaf will eventually be subjected to nearly a dozen different sorting stages along the way to being part of a completed cigar. But now the leaves are packed and sent to a fermentation warehouse, where they will sit for a month or so—depending on the leaf's ultimate purpose—in darkness, sweating out a lot of excess odors and gasses, and undergoing a chemical process that lowers the nicotine level while enhancing the oils.

SORTING

After the first fermentation, the leaves are collected in containers and sent to be sorted into a dizzying array of categories. The leaves usually will be moistened with a fine-mist spray (by a pump bottle or a hose with a nozzle) so their risk of breaking when handled is lessened. Leaves that are to be used as wrappers are treated with much greater respect than those destined for filler and binder, because wrapper leaves are much more delicate. Even if they weren't, they represent the cosmetic aspect of the cigar, which for Cubans is world-famous, so they must be nearly flawless. The wrapper leaves are packed in sturdy containers made of wood or stiff cardboard, while the binder and filler leaves are usually bunched together in bales or stuffed in sacks.

The people responsible for the efficient sorting of the tobacco leaves must have a good eye and many years of experience. All leaves can be placed in any one of a few dozen categories, the criteria for which consider many factors, the most prominent being a leaf's size, color, and texture. Leaves of each category have a predetermined purpose: Some are used for specific cigar sizes, others for particular flavors. None of the categorizations is superfluous.

THE SECOND
FERMENTATION

46

Now that the leaves have been properly sorted and classified, they are sent to another fermentation room, sometimes located in the same place in which they were sorted, to sit again so their pungency can develop further. This fermentation process is a little more extensive than the first, taking up to sixty days or more. The longer they ferment, the more mild they become. So again, the length of the fermentation depends on the ultimate purpose of the leaves.

FACTORIES

After the second fermentation, the leaves are sent to the factories, their last stop before becoming cigars. They go through something of a third fermentation once they arrive, often in the cellars. Depending on the blend the leaves are intended for, this final long-term fermentation period can last up to two years. Cohibas, for example, undergo a very lengthy and concentrated third fermentation, which is one of the secrets of this royal brand.

MOISTENING

When it comes time for a leaf to begin its final journey toward its ultimate purpose, it must first be moistened so it can again be safely handled, which usually is done by subjecting a bunch of leaves to a fine mist, then shaking off the excess. Some bunches are plunged into a shallow pan of water for a second, then quickly removed and shaken off so the water droplets distribute evenly. This is done to "shock" leaves back into life if they have become inordinately dry.

The moistened bunches are hung on large, rolling, cube-shaped wooden frames and put in dark rooms for a few hours. After that they are laid out on sheets and left for up to two days (usually less) while their moisture level regulates to around 30 to 35 percent.

DEVEINING

After the moistening stage, a leaf must be removed of all its obvious veins. This is particularly important for the wrapper leaves, since they of course must look as close to perfect as possible. A woman almost always takes care of this in Cuban factories: It is believed that only women have the delicate touch and skillful dexterity required to properly execute this most vital task. The deveiner lays a single leaf on a piece of cloth in her lap, with the leaf's tip pointing toward her. She patiently flattens the leaf, and then tears out the central vein, slowly at first but with a quick jerk at the end.

A wrapper leaf has then become two half-leaves, each suitable for a single cigar. Needless to say, the larger half-leaves are used for wrapping the larger cigar styles. Often there is a shortage of such leaves, so the larger cigar models are increasingly rare. Even during the best growing seasons, the supply of large-size wrapper leaves is always low relative to those of other sizes.

Piles of the presorted, fully prepared leaves are then stored together in wooden drawers and labeled corresponding to the exact brand and model they are to be used for.

DISTRIBUTION OF LEAVES TO THE ROLLERS

A factory worker sits in front of a scale and weighs out enough leaves to make a certain number of cigars. This person is sure which leaves he or she needs to provide for the roller to create a prescribed blend—for example, which leaves faithfully create a Cohiba Esplendido or a Partagas Lusitania.

After weighing, the leaves are rechecked for moisture. Then, at last, they are sent to the person who possesses what is often thought of as the most romantic job in all of cigar making: the roller.

ROLLING

The rolling stage of a cigar's creation is the one that many think of as the cigar's true "time of birth." Indeed, a cigar really can't be smoked until this point, so perhaps the notion is accurate.

In Havana the entire rolling process usually is done by one person (whereas in some other nations, there often are people who put together the binders and filler, and others who apply the wrappers). The roller begins by putting together the filler leaves according to a predetermined recipe for the blend, or brand, being made that day. If the blend calls for a strong taste, then the roller will be given many *ligero* leaves, harvested from the top of the plant. If on the other hand the cigars require a distinctly mild taste, then there may be only *seco* and *volado* leaves; but most blends require at least a small quantity of *ligero*.

The roller bunches together the filler leaves in what is often called a "book-page" fashion: The leaves are not simply rolled together, but rather arranged in a way reminiscent of a folded hand-held fan, so the cigar's draw will be relatively effortless. For the same reason, the leaves must also be packed relatively loosely, which requires an experienced touch. Tightly packed leaves will make the draw difficult, and the smoking experience will be unpleasant. Conversely, too loose a pack will cause the leaves to burn too quickly, and the taste will be bitter, harsh, and overheated, which will also disappoint.

The filler leaves are bunched together lengthwise, with the strongest leaves in the center. (Some cigars are bunched using a machine for the filler leaves, and then the binder and wrapper leaves are applied by hand, allowing the manufacturer to increase production but still call the cigars *hand-rolled* or *handmade*. Such cigars are referred to as *machine-bunched*.) Then the binder leaf is applied, whose two most important characteristics are its strength, for holding the filler together, and its ability to burn evenly and smoothly. Binder leaves usually are *volados*, which burn quickly, have great physical strength, and have a relatively weak taste.

The embryonic cigar is then placed in a wooden mold that contains enough grooves for about ten cigars. Once all the grooves are occupied, another mold of the same size and shape is fitted on top of the first, trapping the cigars inside. The molds are then subjected to the pressure of a manually operated press that works very much like a vise on a workman's bench; usually more than one mold is pressed at a time. The filler and binder leaves are subjected to this pressure to ensure that they retain their cylindrical shape while the roller applies the wrapper. The cigars usually sit in the mold for about forty-five minutes, although this time can vary from fifteen minutes to a full hour.

Once the cigars are removed from the mold, it is time to apply the wrapper, which is where the greatest skill and care are required: The wrapper leaf accounts not only for a large portion of a cigar's flavor, but also for all of its visual beauty. Therefore the roller who works with wrapper leaves must have the most gentle hands. In Cuba it is not unusual for a student roller to spend up to a year in apprenticeship. Only the most able survive, and even those who do often spend another three or four years working with just the most basic cigar sizes and shapes. The more difficult styles, such as torpedos or figurados, are created only by the masters.

The wrapper leaf, which is actually a half-leaf, is laid on a small wooden board that rests on the desk. The roller gently moistens the wrapper if need be. Then the naked cigar is deposited on the wrapper at an angle, and the wrapper is rolled around it, beginning at the cigar's foot (the end that gets lit), overlapping just slightly. Once it is fully rolled, the roller cuts off the excess with a bare steel blade shaped like a half-moon. Then the roller secures the wrapper with the help of an odorless, tasteless, and basically invisible vegetable-based paste. The head of the cigar is neatly cut, then covered with a "cap"—nothing more than a small circle of tobacco cut from the excess wrapper leaf—which also is applied with the organic paste. The other end of the cigar, sloppy with excess tobacco, is trimmed on the roller's special guillotine to whatever length is required.

TASTING

Once a roller has produced a full lot—usually a hundred—of cigars, the lot is sent to a panel of quality-control experts. These blessed folks are, in essence, getting paid to taste and judge Cuban cigars. They sit in individual booths with pencil and paper and make notes as they puff. Every aspect of the smoking experience is scrutinized, from the cigar's taste and smell to its strength and draw. If an entire panel agree that a cigar from one particular lot is inferior, some of the others from that lot are dissected and analyzed.

The purpose of the panel is not only to assure that the consumer receives the finest product possible, but also that the employees of the industry develop the highest possible standards. If for example the panel decides that it is the quality of the tobacco that has ruined the cigar, anyone from the growers to the selectors may be blamed. If on the other hand the taste of the cigar is pleasant but the draw is too tight, then obviously it is the roller who will need to improve his or her skills. Happily, workers are not often fired from their jobs, but rather taught how to avoid the same mistakes in the future. Workers who are judged to have potential are too hard to come by not to be given the benefit of patience and guidance.

JUDGING THE APPEARANCE

Once a lot of cigars has been okayed by the tasting panel, it is tested again, this time for physical appearance. The person who does this usually inspects about one out of every five cigars per lot. The inspector looks for obvious flaws in the wrapper leaf, squeezes the cigar to make sure the filler has been correctly rolled into place, and compares the cigars to make sure their color, length, and breadth are uniform. Flawed cigars usually are given to factory workers for their personal use, but if the only problem is a slightly imperfect wrapper leaf, the leaf will be removed and the binder-and-filler part sent back for a new wrapper.

FUMIGATION

Finished cigars that have passed their quality tests are subjected to a brief fumigation period, mostly to kill off any remaining parasites or unhatched parasite eggs that might be in the leaves. A colony

54

of tobacco parasites in a large batch of finished cigars can cause huge problems: If undetected, the little pests could wipe out not only the lot of cigars they're presently occupying but any other lots nearby. Think of the small fortune in damage they could easily cause once introduced in a smoke shop, where the owners have invested hundreds of thousands of dollars in stock.

AGING

The storage rooms usually are located in the factory's cellar, and contain thousands and thousands of precious habanos. The cigars are grouped according to brand and style and are left to age, from a few days to a whole year, so their wrapper color and moisture level can "settle" and regulate. The final touches of a Cuban cigar's world-famous flavor are developed here, as a cigar, extremely sensitive to outside aromas, sits in one of these quiet little rooms where the walls, floor, and ceiling have developed the reek of fine tobacco over the span of many years—sometimes more than a century.

COLOR

The fully developed cigars are removed from their aging rooms and sorted according to size and color.

The sizings usually aren't too difficult to determine since the cigars have already been rolled according to a predesigned style and brand. The colors, however, are a different story.

Throughout the many stages of a tobacco leaf, the shade of its brown coloration changes slightly. And, naturally, the same factors that determine a wrapper's color also affect the cigar's overall flavor, so a robusto that bears a certain shade won't taste the same as a robusto that bears another. It is the job of the sorter at this point to make sure the groups of ten, twenty-five, or fifty (and sometimes a hundred, but not often) cigars are unquestionably uniform. He or she takes a roller's lot of a hundred and separates them into piles. On a very general level, there usually are about a half dozen categories, although each can be broken down further. Once a sorter has enough of one kind, he or she passes the batch on to be packaged.

BANDS, BOXES, AND BUNDLES

Cigars usually are packaged either in a flat, shallow box with a lid, or in tied bundles. In both cases workers meticulously arrange the cigars to maintain a level of uniformity. All the bands are lined up perfectly, and the boxed cigars all face exactly the same direction. Nothing would be more embarrassing to these workers than for a consumer to see an open box of Havanas in a display case with one of the cigars turned slightly, with its band off-center. The same is true with the bundles, where the bands on the outer cigars squarely face the people who are looking at them.

Once a complete bundle of habanos has been gathered and properly arranged, it is tied with a handsome satin ribbon. From the ends a bundle of Cuban cigars forms an octagonal shape. A complete box is affixed with the Cuban government's distinctive green-and-white seal (it looks a little like the backs of American paper currency).

READY FOR SALE

Now that a group of Cuban cigars has been grown, fermented, rolled, dressed in decorative brand-name garb, and properly packaged, it is stored at the factory in a cool area until it is shipped. Considering the huge demand for Cuban cigars worldwide, this waiting period is usually a short one. Habanos are sold in all of the economically advanced nations with the singular exception—at the moment—of the United States. In Cuba they are usually offered only by the box, but some retailers will break open one of their smaller boxes and sell the cigars one at a time.

Centuries of development and long hours of hard work have gone into the creation of every habano. Consumers occasionally complain about the relatively high price of the average Cuban cigar, but when one really considers the effort required to create it, the average asking price suddenly seems reasonable.

Today's
Cuban Brands

THERE WAS A TIME WHEN THE CUBAN CIGAR industry produced a tremendous number of brands. As recently as the 1940s, more than two hundred were available. Well over a thousand have been recorded during the past three centuries.

Nowadays about thirty-five major brands (intended mainly for international sale or with long and well-known histories) are left, and a handful of them are relatively new. There are many other brands made in Cuba that do not fall into the nation's premium category; such brands use inferior-quality tobacco and are almost always offered for sale only within the country. Fidel Castro has already said he would like the leaders of the cigar industry to continue developing new brands, a practice that seems to have taken on speed in recent years. Cuaba, for example, was unveiled in 1996, and another new brand is expected to be test-marketed in Spain within the next year.

The following section contains a short discussion of each of the major brands being produced in Cuba. Details about history are prevalent, but there also is information on the main people connected with the brand, the market at which the brand is aimed, the reputed flavor of the brand, and roughly how many styles are being produced at the moment, with information on length and ring gauge (r.g.). These styles are hard to cover with pinpoint accuracy because of the unpredictable nature of the Cuban cigar industry—for example, this week the Cohiba brand will offer fewer than a dozen varieties, but by the time this book is in your hands . . . who knows? A whole new line could have been developed (witness the birth of the Cohiba Siglo series). For complete reliability in this area, it is always best to contact a knowledgeable cigar dealer or distributor who regularly sells habanos or at the very least is very familiar with the Cuban industry.

BELINDA

The Belinda brand was born in 1882, at least in name, when it and three other brand names were registered by an Asturian named Francisco Menéndez Martínez, who had recently bought a factory in Havana and had amassed an impressive knowledge of the Cuban tobacco business. At the time the cigar industry was at a high, and Martínez was making the early Belindas with the finest tobacco leaves he could find; soon the brand had earned a reputation in Europe and the United States. When a lull struck the industry near the turn of the century, the brand lived on, although not with the same vibrancy it had enjoyed previously. Shortly thereafter the brand was sold or leased to a variety of entities, and its production was finally halted in 1960. But the Cuban government's tobacco agency, Cubatobaco, resurrected it in 1987 and has since produced Belindas only by machine, although some are machine-bunched but with hand-rolled wrappers. There are about ten styles, all in a relatively low price range.

BOLIVAR

One of the more affordable Cuban brands, Bolivar also is one of the strongest. The name honors nineteenth-century revolutionary Simon Bolívar (1783–1830), who helped many people in Venezuela, Colombia, Peru, Ecuador, and of course Bolivia, which is named after him, gain their freedom from sovereign Spain. He was born to wealth, and both his parents died when he was very young, leaving him in sole possession of their vast fortune. He visited Europe twice before settling in South America to gather and lead a patriot army, as a general, to break Spain's stranglehold of power. He soon become known as "The Liberator" as well as the "George Washington of South America."

Although Bolívar helped the aforementioned nations gain their freedom, he ruled only Colombia. Even there he eventually became the focal point of suspicion, and in 1830, shortly before his death, he resigned his leadership post following an assassination attempt. Nevertheless, he is remembered fondly as a man who led many people out from under Spain's heavy hand.

His face is hard to miss both on the box label and in the center of the ring. Many sources claim that the brand was established in 1901, but the first record of its existence on paper is from 1921, when the firm of J. F. Rocha y Cía, Inc., registered the name with Cuba's Ministry of Agriculture,

Commerce, and Labor. In 1944 a brand called La Mercantil was merged with Bolivar and subsequently ceased to exist.

There are many varieties of Bolivar, some of which are machine-made or at least machine-bunched, which helps keep them affordable. There are nearly twenty handmade varieties, and almost ten machine-made or -bunched. Sizes range from the tiny demi tasse (4 inches, 30 r.g.) to the coronas gigantes and the tubed Churchills (both 7 inches, 47 r.g.).

CABAÑAS

Produced in the Miguel Fernández Roig factory in Havana, this relatively minor brand dates back to the beginning of the nineteenth century. These days it is made only by machine, although some varieties are machine-bunched with hand-rolled wrappers. There are about a half dozen types, and they are produced almost exclusively for Europe. They are surprisingly full-bodied for the low price.

COHIBA

Probably Cuba's most famous brand, Cohiba is also, surprisingly, one of the youngest, established in 1966 (not 1968, as is often thought) as a private smoke for Castro. Eduardo Rivero Irazarri, who had been rolling cigars professionally since 1957, began making cigars for himself using a unique blend of his own design. A few of these cigars were given to one of Castro's personal bodyguards, and it wasn't long before the president got wind, literally, of their tantalizing and gentle aroma. He recruited Rivero as his personal roller, at first making the cigars in secret; Castro would either smoke them himself or give them away as diplomatic gifts. Cohiba was commercialized in 1982 and has since become the keystone of the Cuban cigar industry, although Montecristo remains its bestseller. The name comes from the ancient Taino Indian word for tobacco.

The leaves used to make Cohibas are the best that Cuba has to offer, taken from the fields of the legendary El Corojo and Hoyo de Monterrey regions. Perhaps the key to Cohiba's flavor is that the leaves are fermented three times rather than the usual two. Supposedly only a handful of people know the formula used to produce the effective Cohiba blend. Rivero, incidentally, who could be considered the father of the brand, is still alive and well and making cigars in Havana, although in 1970 he left the factory where the Cohibas were produced. An article about him was published in the autumn 1995 issue of *Cigar Aficionado.*

When Cohiba was commercialized in 1982, only three types were offered, all Castro favorites: the lancero (Castro's main preference), the corona especial, and the panetela. In 1989 three more types were introduced: the exquisito, the robusto, and the esplendido. The latter could very well be the most celebrated cigar in the world despite its hefty price tag. Then in late 1992, Cohiba unveiled five more styles, issued under the names Siglo I, II, III, IV, and V, measuring between 4 and 6⅝ inches (10 and 16.7 centimeters) and ring sizes from 40 to 46. And there has been some talk of offering a handful of new Cohiba styles, including a torpedo. The series supposedly was created to celebrate Christopher Columbus's discovery of the Americas, Cuba, cigars, and whatever else he and his men stumbled across at the time. However, many people believe its actual purpose was to replace certain popular Davidoff sizes that were no longer produced in Cuba after the Davidoff company moved to the Dominican Republic.

CUABA

One of Cuba's most recent creations, the Cuaba line was produced, according to Rich Perelman's *Perelman's Pocket Cyclopedia of Havana Cigars,* to reflect the growing mid-1990s interest in shaped cigars. There are only four models at the moment, all of the figurado shape and entirely handmade, mainly because it is very difficult to create the shape by machine. The name of the brand comes from the Taino Indian word that seems to refer to the bush the Tainos used to light their own crude cigars.

The Cuaba blend was created by Carlos Izquierdo González, who had worked at the Briones Montoto factory since the late forties and undoubtedly is one of the most talented rollers in the world. In an article on the brand in the March-April 1997 issue of *Cigar Aficionado*, González said that he had been trying for many years to convince the factory to make figurados, since the production of this shape had all but died in Cuba save for a single Partagas model called the Presidente.

The brand was premiered and test-marketed only in Great Britain, where it apparently has been very well received; Cuba plans to eventually offer it worldwide. Its flavor, by González's design, starts off strong but mellows toward the end.

DIPLOMATICOS

A fairly young brand, the Diplomaticos line was introduced in 1966, mainly to attract French smokers. It was supposed to be a sort of bargain substitute for the Montecristo line, which has always been pricey. There are not as many Diplomatico varieties—seven at the time of this writing—as there are Montecristos, but their quality is nearly compatible. For the price, Diplomaticos offer an attractive product with a rich, full-bodied flavor. American smokers may recognize the distinctive carriage design on the label as similar to that of a brand sold legally in the States called Licenciados.

EL REY DEL MUNDO

A very old Cuban brand, first established in 1848 under the capable direction of Antonio Allones. At that time it was considered one of the finest cigars Cuba had to offer, and its price reflected confidence in its quality. Its taste has been modified somewhat through the years: In its early stages El Reys were quite powerful, but they are now rather mild. Most are beautifully constructed, and their dark and oily wrappers are a feast for the eyes.

The phrase *El Rey del Mundo* translates to "King of the World," proof of the confidence this brand inspired. Today there are about a dozen varieties coming out of Cuba, the majority completely hand-made. The name has also been licensed to a cigar manufacturer in Honduras, whose El Reys are slightly more bitter than the Cuban variety and do not possess the same breathtaking workmanship.

FONSECA

The birth and subsequent rise to popularity of this brand can be attributed largely to its founder, Francisco E. Fonseca. He set up a factory in Havana in 1891, and by the early twentieth century the name was officially registered. While Francisco undoubtedly was a fine businessman, his most valuable talents in the cigar business probably were his ability to choose fine tobacco and his undying desire to please fellow smokers. He would go to great lengths to accumulate consumer opinions about his products and then to make whatever adjustments he felt were necessary. In its early days, Fonseca was produced mainly for private affairs and smoking societies, but it became more widespread when word of its impeccable quality got around. The Fonseca cigars of today are immensely popular in Spain and Switzerland.

The Fonseca name has also been licensed to a manufacturer in the Dominican Republic. It is easy to tell the Cuban Fonsecas from the Dominicans, even from across the room: The

Cubans come wrapped in white tissue paper. At present Cuba only produces about a half dozen Fonseca types.

GISPERT

Gispert was first blended in 1940. At that time all varieties were entirely handmade and produced right in the famous Pinar del Río region; now they are offered only in machine-made varieties, with one variety's wrapper hand-rolled. Gisperts are relatively short, have medium girth, and are mild, but can become bitter more quickly than the average smoker might prefer. Fans of this brand may find it hard to obtain: It could very well be one of Cuba's dying brands, with such a tiny following that it may soon become too impractical to produce.

HOYO DE MONTERREY

Sometime around 1860, José Gener began growing tobacco leaves in a particularly fertile valley—prime for tobacco due to drainage from the surrounding hills—in the famed Vuelta Abajo region, which became known as Hoyo de Monterrey, or "valley of Monterrey." Today this region specializes in binder and filler tobacco. Gener went on to establish the Hoyo de Monterrey brand in 1865, and it survives as one of Cuba's finest. There are over a dozen handmade varieties, and a dozen more are made with the help of machines. Hoyos offer smokers a light, easy flavor and an attractive, light wrapper. A new addition to the Hoyo line was established in the early 1970s, dubbed the Le Hoyo series, which are a bit stronger than other Hoyos.

H. UPMANN

The history of the world-famous H. Upmann brand reads almost like a novel, with highs and lows and, ultimately, a relatively happy ending. The brand was born in 1844 when two brothers, Herman and August Upmann, opened a cigar store in Havana. They had arrived from Germany the year before, loaded with money and ambition and looking for fresh opportunities. The Upmanns were from a successful banking family, and they continued with their banking endeavors in Cuba while dabbling in the increasingly popular cigar market. The initial Upmann varieties were made only from tobacco grown in the renowned Vuelta Abajo region. Soon the brothers' cigar business was moving along so smoothly that their banking ventures became a lesser priority. Upmann cigars were being sold not only in Cuba, but in the international market as well.

Herman Upmann died in 1894, but the brand did not. Two of Herman's three sons went to Cuba shortly after their father's death to take over the business, guided by the capable supervision of the still-surviving August. Eventually he returned to Germany and left the cigar business in the control of his nephews.

The industry took a nosedive in the waning years of the nineteenth century, and the Upmanns almost found themselves out of business, but a boom early in the twentieth century saved them. Unfortunately the outbreak of World War I unleashed a Pandora's box of problems for the German-born Upmanns, and by 1922 they were finished in Cuba, and all their assets were swiftly liquidated and sold. Herman Jr. died in 1925, and his brother Albert moved to the United States.

A London-based company purchased the Upmann factory during the liquidation and went to great pains to keep the brand alive. But a variety of problems riddled their efforts, and in 1936 Upmann was sold again, this time to Menéndez, García y Cía, the same firm responsible for the creation of Montecristo. This firm knew cigars and the cigar business better than any of Upmann's previous owners, and soon the brand was on its way to a triumphant return. In 1944, to celebrate its hundredth anniversary, a new factory was opened. The market for Upmann broadened, with demands pouring in from virtually every major cigar-smoking country in the world.

Through the years and various ownerships, Upmann has won a variety of respected awards; and the name continues to impress cigar lovers everywhere. There are dozens of varieties produced in Cuba, some handmade, some machine-made. There also are Upmanns made in the Dominican Republic, but none possess the delicious flavor of the habanos.

JOSÉ L. PIEDRA

One of the smaller and lesser-known brands, José L. Piedra also is one of the least expensive to come from Cuba, and is sold both nationally and internationally. All half dozen varieties are machine-made but with hand-rolled wrappers, which are dark and not as oily as those of other brands. Piedra cigars also are not as lovingly constructed as most other habanos, so they have a more pedestrian appearance. Nevertheless they are a good value for the money, providing a swift and pleasing smoke, with a fairly strong and somewhat bitter taste.

JUAN LÓPEZ

Although now one of the smallest brands in Cuba, Juan López has a rich and impressive history. The factory that first produced it was established in the early 1870s by Juan López Díaz, a connoisseur of fine cigars who had a talent for creating blends that pleased even the most discerning smokers. In 1876 he created a new brand, modestly named it La Flor de Juan López, and used only the finest Vuelta Abajo leaves available at the time. By the turn of the century the brand had developed a shining reputation. Juan died in the early 1900s, but his namesake cigars were kept alive after being purchased by an independent tobacco firm.

Today Juan López does not enjoy much of its former glory: Production has shrunk to only a handful of varieties, and there are rumors that it will further shrink until only the corona and petit corona types remain. Nevertheless it enjoys something of a cult following in Spain and is known for its easy draw and mild aroma.

LA CORONA

This brand has a long and fascinating history but does not maintain the same popularity as it once did. In 1845 the owners of a cigar factory in Havana launched a new brand and named it La Corona, "the crown." Like so many other successful Cuban brands, the initial La Coronas were made only from the finest tobacco leaves, and it wasn't long before the demand nearly exceeded supply.

In 1882 the brand was sold, then resold, and eventually ended up in the hands of two experienced manufacturers. La Corona then took off like a bullet, and by the end of the century it was one of the most recognized and respected brands in the world. The workforce in the factory grew to unprecedented size, and by 1910 there were nearly forty thousand cigars being produced every day.

La Corona's reign finally began to sag when financial troubles struck the United States, which had long been one of its most reliable markets, during the Great Depression. By 1933 the number of cigars the United States was taking had decreased by nearly 75 percent. To save money, La Corona had to make drastic and immediate changes. One of the most severe was moving operations to Trenton, New Jersey, where cigars meant for worldwide sale (those to be sold to the Cuban people would still be made domestically) would be rolled using the same high-quality Cuban leaves.

Today the factory that once produced the domestic product still stands in Havana and continues to make fine cigars, including the La Coronas. The factory was named after the famous La Corona brand at its inception but was later renamed during Castro's nationalization process to the Miguel Fernández Roig factory. Roig was a workers' leader who was murdered at the factory in 1948, a time of violent unrest between labor and management.

There are about twenty varieties of La Corona, all with fairly strong flavor, and all made with the aid of machines, about half with hand-rolled wrappers. They are sold almost exclusively in Europe. There also is a small line of Dominican La Coronas, all of which are handmade.

LA FLOR DE CANO

This increasingly rare brand was born in 1891 by brothers Tomás and Juan Cano, who had established a factory in Havana seven years earlier. In the beginning, the brand was immensely popular, with its aromatic flavor and neat construction. But for whatever reason its popularity began to wane, and now there are fewer than a dozen varieties, half of which are machine-bunched. In spite of their scarcity, they still carry a devoted following in Great Britain and the Middle East.

LA FLOR DEL CANEY

One of Cuba's relatively minor brands, established only in the 1970s, and produced more or less entirely by machine. It is a powerful smoke and therefore not recommended for amateurs. Most varieties are under 5½ inches (14 centimeters) long and have a ring gauge of less than 40. Perfect for those quick lunchtime smokes.

LA GLORIA CUBANA

Two gentlemen by the names of José Fernández Rocha and José Rodríguez Fernández, who owned a Havana tobacco firm (J. F. Rocha y Cía, Inc.) in the early part of the twentieth century, established this brand in 1920. Their vision was to forever link the brand to the finest tobacco Cuba had to offer, and their efforts were further aided by the relentless promotional work of Pepín Fernández, the owner of another legendary brand, Romeo y Julieta. La Gloria became successful almost instantly. Rocha had died by the forties, but the brand continued its reign as one of Cuba's premier blends. Manufacture did slow after Castro's nationalization, but the brand never died off completely. Its main market in the old days was Europe, Spain in particular, and today it is one of the most familiar and respected brands in the world.

There are a half dozen styles being produced in Cuba, all handmade. They are characterized by a peppery but subtle and earthy flavor and a rich, tantalizing aroma. Another dozen styles are being produced in the United States and the Dominican Republic. Although Cuba's version probably is superior to its American counterpart in the minds of most smokers, the latter should not be ignored. For smokers who are unable to acquire the Cubans, the American and Dominican La Glorias are strongly recommended. It is this author's opinion that these La Gloria Cubanas are among the finest non-Cuban cigars available in the world.

77

LOS STATOS DE LUXE

One of the smaller Cuban brands, Los Statos de Luxe was created by the Martínez brothers of Martínez y Cía. The handsome box design features a spread eagle behind a small, *M*-shaped shield bearing a burning torch. Most of the cigars in this line are relatively small (none much over 5½ inches, or 14 centimeters), and all are made either entirely by machine or machine-bunched with hand-rolled wrappers. They are relatively affordable and offer rich, full-bodied flavor.

MONTECRISTO

Easily the best-selling of all Cuban brands, Montecristo began its life as nothing more than a variety of the H. Upmann brand, the H. Upmann Montecristo Selection in 1935. It was conceived by two gentlemen who had bought Upmann and wanted to extend the existing assortment. Shortly before World War II, Montecristo became a brand all its own and was given its distinctive brown-and-white ring and yellow-and-red box design. The name Montecristo as well as the use of swords and fleur-de-lis on the box are believed to have been inspired by the 1844 Alexandre Dumas novel *The Count of Monte Cristo.*

There are around a dozen styles of Montecristo, with the No. 2 and the No. 4 probably the most popular. All Montecristos are hand-rolled, have a strong and earthy flavor, and a fairly dark wrapper. They are by far the most beloved Cuban cigars in Europe.

PARTAGAS

Perhaps no other man had as powerful an impact on the Cuban cigar industry in the nineteenth century as Jaime Partagás Ravelo, a wise and ambitious businessman who had his first shop up and running by the late 1820s. Not long after that he was buying up parcels of land in the Pinar del Río province.

In 1845 he launched a new brand, naming it after himself. As with everything else he did, he set remarkably high standards for the Partagas line. He insisted they be made with the best leaves and rolled by only the most skilled hands. One of his greatest characteristics was the fearless way he deviated from many of the traditional cigar-making processes in the spirit of experimentalism and the eternal search for new directions, constantly applying fresh ideas to farming, curing, fermenting, and blending. He also focused some of his pioneering energies on advertising and packaging.

79

His hard work paid off: The Partagas cigar soon became known as a work of art. Once Jaime realized there was a broad range of smokers, with a broad range of tastes to match, he expanded his selection until he was convinced he had something for everyone. In an effort to keep his workers happy, he introduced the reader: the person responsible for combating boredom among the factory workers by reading to them from a book or newspaper.

Partagás's cigars continued to rise in popularity all over the world. Jaime also produced his own line of cigarettes and pipe tobacco. The more success he had, it seemed, the more he wanted. Then in 1868 he was shot while returning to his home, and died as a result of the wounds some weeks later. His family kept the business going for a while, but, much to their good fortune, they sold it just before the tobacco industry hit its low point in the closing years of the nineteenth century.

80

The Partagas products eventually ended up in the hands of another visionary in the tobacco business, Ramón Cifuentes Llano, who further improved the line and bought up a few other brands as well. Cifuentes died in 1938, leaving his business to his family. Shortly after World War II they began making some cigars by machine, which may have made many workers unhappy, but also improved the level of production. By the time Castro enacted nationalization in the sixties, Partagas was one of the giants of the industry.

Today Partagas is still one of the most respected and beloved brands in the world. And, in the true tradition of its founder, it features a dazzling variety of styles: There are well over sixty being produced in Cuba alone, and a well-known Dominican line as well. About eighteen are entirely handmade, another two dozen are entirely machine-made, and the rest are machine-bunched with hand-rolled wrappers.

POR LARRAÑAGA

It is generally believed that this is the oldest extant Cuban brand, born in 1834 by Ignacio Larrañaga, and going on to certain fame after being mentioned in the Rudyard Kipling poem "The Betrothed." (This is the same poem, incidentally, that spawned the now-famous—and, many would be quick to point out, politically incorrect—line "A woman is only a woman, but a good cigar is a smoke.") While there is little doubt that the Por Larrañaga brand enjoyed a certain measure of popularity in the nineteenth century, its following has shrunk considerably since then. Today there are very few varieties being produced—about a dozen with only one or two being handmade—but they are rich and full-bodied with a mildly sweet tang. Travelers to Cuba probably won't have much trouble finding them. The Dominican Republic also produces a Por Larrañaga brand, which is caringly blended and pleasing to the senses.

81

PUNCH

A very old Cuban brand, Punch was created in 1840 by a man named Juan Valle. He intended it to be a product for the British market, and the name came from that of a popular British humor magazine. (Famed Winnie-the-Pooh creator A. A. Milne worked for many years on its editorial staff.) From 1874 to 1940 the Punch brand bounced around from owner to owner until it finally ended up in the firm Fernández Palicio y Cía. By World War II it had earned a devoted following in much of Europe, particularly in Spain and Great Britain.

Today the Punch brand continues to draw admirers the world over, still particularly in Europe. It has a reputation for a mild but full-bodied flavor, most models are reasonably priced, and there are many to choose from. Of the nearly forty types that Punch produces in Cuba, about half are made entirely by hand. There also is a Honduran Punch line (pun not intended), and like the Cuban counterparts there are quite a few shapes and sizes available.

QUAI D'ORSAY

A small brand created in 1970, Quai d'Orsay is produced only for the French government's singular tobacco firm La Société Nationale d'Exploitation Industriel de Tabac et Allumettes (SEITA); the name of the brand comes from that of a well-known bridge in Paris. There are five styles, ranging from the Coronas Claro (5½ inches, 42 r.g.) to the Imperiales (7 inches, 47 r.g.); all are handmade and feature a mild aroma.

QUINTERO

One of the more interesting success stories in the Cuban cigar business, the Quintero brand was created in 1924 when Agustin Quintero and his brothers opened a tiny factory in Cienfuegos, which lies not in Havana but rather in the Las Villas region of southern Cuba. In spite of Quintero's remoteness from the heartland of the Cuban cigar industry, he worked diligently to make his namesake brand as worthy as any of the cigars made in Havana, and the brand developed a solid reputation both in Cuba and abroad.

Today Quintero's production is somewhat limited: There are only a few entirely handmade models, and another dozen that are made with the aid of machines. Nevertheless, the Quintero name still enjoys a cult following and has upheld its standing as a cigar of mild but rich and full-bodied flavor.

RAFAEL GONZALEZ

Although made in relatively small numbers, the Rafael Gonzalez cigars are adored and respected by many discerning smokers. The brand was created in 1928 by Márquez Rafael González with Great Britain in mind, and the price was intentionally kept reasonable (and is still reasonable today) so the cigars could be enjoyed by everyone, not just the elite. It is generally accepted that this brand was the first to make a cigar in the lonsdale size, supposedly as a sort of present for the Earl of Lonsdale. On the box is the advice that a smoker should either smoke the cigars immediately after purchase or let them age in a humidor for about a year. Gonzalez cigars are known for their mild, subtle, and rich flavor, which has been likened to that of Montecristo, and they burn well and are artfully constructed. There are a half dozen handmade brands, and a couple more made by machine, and they are among the best Cuban cigars one can get for the money.

RAMON ALLONES

The Ramon Allones brand has enjoyed a steadily moderate level of success. The father of the brand, Ramón Allones himself, came to Cuba from

Galicia, Spain, in 1837 along with his brother Antonio, and by 1846 had registered the brand that bore his name. He was a natural in the cigar industry, and his masterful blends went on to win many fans in Europe and North and South America. His cigars were so adored in his homeland that he was given official permission to use the Royal House of Spain's coat of arms on his cigar boxes. He was the first to colorfully decorate a cigar box, a practice that has since become standard, and also the first to utilize the now-common 8-9-8 stacking style inside the boxes. His cigars and their handsome cases were admired by everyone, from proletarians to imperials. As his success grew, he expanded his business, buying up a few other brands in the process.

In 1911 the Allones business was sold to overseas investors, and again in 1927 to the owners of the Partagas brand, Ramon Cifuentes y Cía. Since then the Partagas people have worked hard to keep the famous Allones brand alive and well. Today the boxes are as handsome and decorative as ever, and the cigars are offered in about twenty different models. Roughly half are entirely handmade, the rest either made entirely by machine or machine-bunched with hand-rolled wrappers. The smaller varieties are said to be a bit milder than the larger, but all carry a rich and fairly strong flavor, and are not recommended for the beginner. The Dominican equivalent of this brand is also very aromatic.

ROMEO Y JULIETA

One of the most famous and beloved Cuban brands in the world, Romeo y Julieta came from humble beginnings. It was created in 1873 by two Spaniards, Inocencio Álvarez Rodríguez and José Mannin García, small-time cigar manufacturers, with a tiny factory on San Rafael Street in Havana. But their stint at the lower levels of the industry didn't last long. They tirelessly devoted themselves to the quality of every aspect of their product, and were particularly discriminating in their choice of leaves. It wasn't long before even the pickiest smokers became loyal followers.

García left the partnership in 1886, and Álvarez carried on awhile. But by 1903 the Romeo y Julieta line was in the hands of José Rodríguez Fernández, known by most as Don Pepín. He was as native to the cigar business as a fish is to water, and under his skillful direction the Romeo y Julieta cigar went from local fame to international fortune. Pepín was an ardent believer in the value of marketing and promotion. A former overseas sales manager of cigars with many years of experience, he had no trouble getting the word of his product into the collective conscience of consumers worldwide. Soon he had a new factory, which was named after the flagship brand, and was producing twenty million cigars per year with a staff of over a thousand workers. He also wisely expanded the Romeo y Julieta selection to make sure he would please smokers of all tastes. Notably, it was this brand that first produced the now-standard Churchill style, named after former British Prime Minister Winston Churchill and in fact designed to his preference. Churchill was, as many cigar historians are well aware, an unswerving devotee to the cigars of Cuba.

Part of Pepín's success no doubt can be credited to his elegant, cheerful, and gentlemanly persona. He was a much-loved figure in international cigar circles, always willing to lend his vast knowledge of the business to anyone who requested it. He died in 1954 at the age of eighty-eight, a legend in the fast-paced and highly competitive world of the Cuban cigar business.

Today the Romeo y Julieta brand carries on Don Pepín's tradition by offering an enormous array of models—nearly two dozen made entirely by hand, and roughly another forty made with the aid of machines, about half of which are machine-bunched with hand-rolled wrappers, and are made exclusively in the Briones Montoto (formerly Romeo y Julieta) factory. The larger sizes can be fairly expensive, even in Cuba, but the smaller varieties are usually affordable. The flavor of the average Romeo y Julieta seems to capture the very essence of the word *smooth:* not harsh or overpowering, perfect for any time of day or night, and undoubtedly are among the finest cigars in the world.

SAINT LUIS REY

Saint Luis Rey began in the late 1930s upon request of two British tobacco importers, Michael Keyser and Nathan Silverstone. The cigars were blended to be particularly powerful, although they also offered an earthy, pleasing aroma. They have always been an exceptional value, affordable to the common man.

Some confusion over the name's origin has surrounded the brand. On one hand there is the possibility that it was inspired by the Thornton Wilder play *The Bridge of San Luis Rey,* but there also is a San Luis sector in Cuba's famed Vuelta Abajo growing region.

Today the brand has a very limited production run. Europe is still its main market, and there are only a half dozen models offered, all handmade.

SANCHO PANZA

Featuring a painting of jolly Sancho Panza, squire to Don Quixote, on the box, this brand is among Cuba's oldest. It was created sometime in the early 1850s by a gentleman named Emilio Ahmsted. The same firm that owned the Allones brand took possession of it in 1920, but then sold it seven years later. In 1931 it was sold again, this time to the Rey del Mundo company, where it remained until 1960. Today it is produced only in the Briones Montoto factory—where the Romeo y Julieta line is also made—in fairly limited quantities: Only a half dozen models are offered, and the main market is Europe, particularly France and Spain.

The Panza line is known for its mildness. Some have cited a salty tang to the flavor, and others have complained about a tight draw and poor construction. Still, Panza has acquired a loyal following, and there is some talk of expanding the selection in the near future. One of the largest cigars produced in Cuba belongs to this group: the absurdly sized Sanchos, at 9¼ inches (23.5 centimeters) with a ring gauge of 47.

SIBONEY

Like Quai d'Orsay, Siboney is a recent brand produced only for a government-run tobacco monopoly, in this case Austria's. Only a single model is currently offered: the Especial, which measures 6 inches (15.2 centimeters), has a ring gauge of 38, and features a mild flavor. And also like the Quai d'Orsay line, it is made only in the Briones Montoto factory, in very small numbers.

TRINIDAD

This was once the great mystery cigar of our time, mainly because so many unanswered questions surrounded it. It was first produced in 1991, reportedly as a sort of updated Cohiba in the sense that it was intended only as a gift from the Cuban government (how Cohiba started). Castro even said in an interview that he had no knowledge of the Trinidad, denying reports that he had ordered its creation. However, their factory's director said they had been created specifically for Fidel, mainly as diplomatic gifts that only he could give away. In any case, only a handful of people in the world had ever

even seen one until Marvin Shanken, publisher of
Cigar Aficionado, held a "dinner of the century" in
Paris in October 1994 at which all 164 guests were
treated to a bona fide Trinidad before their meal. In
May 1997, a Swiss cigar enthusiast paid $11,400
for a box of twenty-five Trinidads, the first time any
had been offered commercially.

Only a single model was initially produced, a
copy in size of Cohiba's famous Lancero model,
with a length of 7½ inches (19 centimeters) and a
ring gauge of 38. The cap even bears the familiar
twisted pigtail. The wrapper leaf, however, is a bit
darker than any used on Cohibas, and the flavor is
supposedly a bit stronger. The production run of
Trinidads is very small—reportedly only two
thousand per month—and are made only in the
El Laguito factory. They are usually offered in boxes
of a hundred, although boxes of fifty and twenty-
five are not unknown. The ring is a simple yet
elegant gold band with the word *Trinidad* printed
in slim, black capital letters and bordered above
and below by a single black line. Although the blend
of the Trinidad is most certainly a secret, one El
Laguito employee hinted that it is essentially the
same as the Cohiba Lancero except with a darker
wrapper and an extended fermentation stage.

When I casually inquired about the Trinidad brand during my research trip to Cuba, no one—from rollers to farmers—seemed to know anything about it. One particularly high-ranking manager in the Pinar del Río region seemed uncomfortable with the topic and quickly steered the conversation elsewhere.

In March 1998, cigar lovers in Canada and Mexico were privileged to have a new version of the famed Trinidad—the Fundadores (7.25 inches long with a 40 ring gauge)—released commercially. Connoisseurs bought them up as quickly as Habanos S.A. could make them. Once again Castro and his cigar tsars proved they could be as shrewd and as clever as any American capitalists. They created a mystique around a cigar simply by withholding it from the public (as they did with Cohiba), then, when curiosity reached a fever pitch, they began offering the brand in limited quantities.

Habanos S.A. stated that production of the Trinidad Fundadores was to be limited to about five hundred thousand cigars during its first year of release, but that production would very likely increase after that. Additional sizes were also being considered.

In order to further publicize and celebrate the release of the new Trinidad, a gala dinner was held in Havana in late February, where samples of the new smoke were offered to all guests. Noted figures both in the cigar industry and from other circles attended the occasion. Many were American, including actor Matt Dillon. Castro himself was also in attendance. He autographed five large humidors containing 101 Fundadores each that were made specially for evening. Afterward they were auctioned off to raise money for Cuba's public-health system: The total take for all five was over three hundred thousand dollars.

TROYA

Once a fairly popular and widely produced brand, Troya has now all but disappeared. There are only two models left, both made either entirely by machine or with hand-rolled wrappers. They are produced only in the Heroes de Moncada factory. The name was inspired by the Trojan War as depicted in Homer's *Iliad*.

VEGAS ROBAINA

One of the few new Cuban brands produced in the last five years, Vegas Robaina honors one of Cuba's most accomplished tobacco farmers, Don Alejandro Robaina, Sr. Robaina, who was seventy-eight at the time of the brand's launch in 1997, is the head of one of the most renowned tobacco-growing families in Cuba. He has been in charge of the family plantation since nearly a decade before Fidel Castro came to power. His family's history of tobacco farming dates back to the mid–nineteenth century.

To celebrate the birth of the new brand, Habanos S.A. held gala dinners in Barcelona and Madrid in June 1997. Naturally, there were plenty of Vegas Robaina samples for all attendees. The brand is made with filler tobacco grown in the Pinar del Río, particularly the San Luis area. The wrapper leaves come only from Alejandro's crop, and all cigars are rolled at the famous H. Upmann factory. They bear a handsome brown-and-gold band with a royal *R* in the center.

At the outset, Habanos S.A.'s plan was to test market the new brand only in Spain, basing their future strategy on how the brand fared in this limited arena. Five sizes were offered: Don Alejandro (double corona, 7⅝ inches, 49 r.g.), Únicos (piramide, 6⅛ inches, 52 r.g.), Clásico (lonsdale, 6½ inches, 42 r.g.), Familiar (corona gorda, 5½ inches, 42 r.g.), and Famosos (hermoso no. 4, 5 inches, 48 r.g.). The blend is strong and rather peppery in character, and even Don Alejandro himself admitted that the leaves were still a bit young at the time of the brand's initial presentation, but that they would improve with time.

VEGUEROS

This is a very new brand that has grown in popularity with astonishing speed. It was humbly created in the only cigar-rolling factory in the Pinar del Río region of Cuba, where its reasonable price (a dollar apiece for the lancero size when I was in Cuba in July 1997) and hearty aroma quickly earned it a strong local reputation. Soon it began turning up in tourist shops across the country.

Eventually Vegueros made it onto the international market, where it also met with great success. When I visited Canada in February 1998 I found Vegueros in every smoke shop I visited. It was offered in a variety of shapes and sizes, from the little petit corona five-packs to the Cohiba Lancero–styled Vegueros Special. It has been compared to Cohiba in terms of taste, although it is a little spicier and becomes bitter more rapidly. Nevertheless, there is a very good chance that this tasty and remarkably affordable cigar will soon become one of the prized features of the industry.

The United States–Cuba
Trade Embargo

IN CASE YOU HAVEN'T HEARD, A TRADE
embargo exists between the United States and
Cuba, and American smokers are unable to
legally obtain cigars, not to mention all other
items, of Cuban origin. The embargo has been in
effect for more than thirty years and was enacted
by President John F. Kennedy after a brief period
of stormy relations between the American government and the new Castro regime.

Before Castro came to power, Cuba and the
United States had what could easily be called a
healthy trade relationship. To draw revenues, Batista
had groomed Cuba to be the premier tourist attrac-

tion of the Caribbean, and thousands of Americans visited the island every year. American businesses had a multitude of interests in Cuba: The Ford Motor Company had over thirty-five dealerships, Sears Roebuck had more than a half dozen retail shops, and American-owned entities controlled almost 90 percent of the telephone and electric companies, not to mention most of the railway and petroleum operations. America was taking more than half of Cuba's total exports by the end of the fifties, and about three-fourths of Cuba's imports were American.

Then Castro overthrew Batista and restructured the basic political structure to fit in with his own communist beliefs. All the rules changed, and relations between Cuba and the United States plummeted at breakneck speed: In October 1960 the United States implemented a series of restrictive controls on all exports to Cuba; in January 1961 they officially broke off all diplomatic relations; in April 1961 the ill-fated Bay of Pigs Invasion took place; and in December 1961 Castro abolished all forms of democracy. Infuriated, the Organization of American States (OAS) suspended Cuba's membership in January 1962.

But the new Cuban leader would not swerve from his course. So on February 3, 1962, President

John F. Kennedy signed an embargo banning all trade between Cuba and the United States, to weaken Cuba's communist government and punish Castro for refusing to compensate American businesses for the more than one billion dollars worth of property he had seized. From that moment on, cigar smokers in the United States could not legally obtain any tobacco products made in Cuba (except for Kennedy himself, who often received them through diplomatic pouches).

As with many other laws or proclamations, the Cuban trade embargo has undergone some minor alterations since its inception. One of the most notable influences was a resolution in July 1975 by the Organization of American States to reestablish trade relations with Cuba: Any member could again trade freely with Cuba if they so desired. Many nations jumped at the opportunity, but the United States was not one of them. However, a month later the United States permitted foreign subsidiaries of U.S. companies to trade with Cuba, albeit under certain conditions and only with a license from the Treasury Department.

In September 1977 the United States and Cuba each established their own interests sections in the capitals of the other's country, sponsored by the embassies of third-party countries. No pure-bred American embassy has existed in Cuba since the early sixties.

The eighties were a relatively quiet time between America and Cuba. There were of course the occasional incidents—the U.S. removal of Cuban forces from Grenada in October 1983 and the return of the Mariel boatlift refugees in December 1984—but nothing major took place that would affect the embargo. But in October 1992, President George Bush signed the Cuban Democracy Act, the brainchild of New Jersey Democratic Representative Robert Torricelli, which further tightened the embargo. Under its two main terms, foreign subsidiaries of U.S. companies were no longer allowed to engage in trade with Cuba (essentially a reversal of the 1975 resolution), and ships that entered a Cuban harbor to engage in trade were forbidden to then enter a U.S. harbor for at least six months.

Another ballast to the embargo came with the Helms-Burton Act, signed into law on March 12, 1996, by President Bill Clinton in response to the Cuban government's shooting down of two civilian aircraft that had violated Cuban airspace. The purpose of this act, much the same as the original embargo's, was to increase economic pressure on Cuba by discouraging foreign investment, most notably through the use of U.S. properties expropriated by Castro's government during nationalization. In 1998 President Clinton agreed to ease some of the restrictions concerning travel to Cuba, prompted by the Pope's historic visit to the island earlier in the year. Clinton lifted the total ban on direct flights to Cuba from the United States, and also increased the amount of cash Cuban-American citizens were allowed to send or bring to relatives each year. But alas, this obviously did little to help American cigar smokers.

Many foreign nations that are friendly with the United States but also enjoy free trade with Cuba were angered by the Helms-Burton Act, feeling as though America was attempting to govern world trade. But many of the provisions in the act are subject to suspension by the U.S. president, and thus far diplomatic relations between America and its allies have not suffered.

As with any other conflict, the Cuban embargo has its supporters and its opponents. Among the opponents are droves of American businessmen—including many in the cigar industry, although not, of course, the manufacturers—who see abundant opportunities in the former Jewel of the Caribbean. There also is a fair share of Cuban natives who are tired of communism and are ready to begin a journey into the potentially prosperous world of free enterprise. As an American visitor in Castro's Cuba, I have to admit I was quite surprised by the number of people who, both openly and in whispers, said they were eager to subscribe to a more capitalistic way of life because they felt they had given communism a chance and were growing increasingly disappointed by it. Whether capitalism is the answer to Cuba's problems or not can of course only be speculated, but there seem to be quite a few weary Cubans who are ready to give it a try.

In November 1992 the United Nations General Assembly approved a resolution calling for an end to the U.S. embargo, supported for a variety of reasons, perhaps most widely for humanitarian ones: Many Cuban citizens are suffering under appalling living conditions. And hundreds of thousands of Cuban refugees in Miami and elsewhere are waiting to return to their homeland; many have family members in Cuba whom they have not seen since their departure.

On the other hand, there are foreign nations that are dependent on Cuba to some degree for

A typical farmhouse.

Above: Leaves hanging to sweat out their excess moisture.

Right: Bundles of wrapper leaves ready for fermen-tation.

These cigars in their molds have had their binder leaves applied, but not the wrapper leaves, which aren't added until the roller is sure that the leaves will hold together.

Unfinished cigars are kept under pressure in molds, with the help of cigar presses, for thirty minutes to an hour.

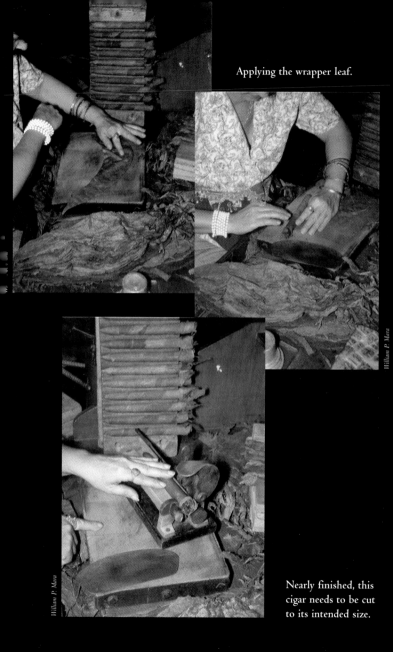

Applying the wrapper leaf.

William P. Mara

William P. Mara

Nearly finished, this cigar needs to be cut to its intended size.

Applying bands . . .

. . . and finally
ribbons.

William P. Mara

William P. Mara

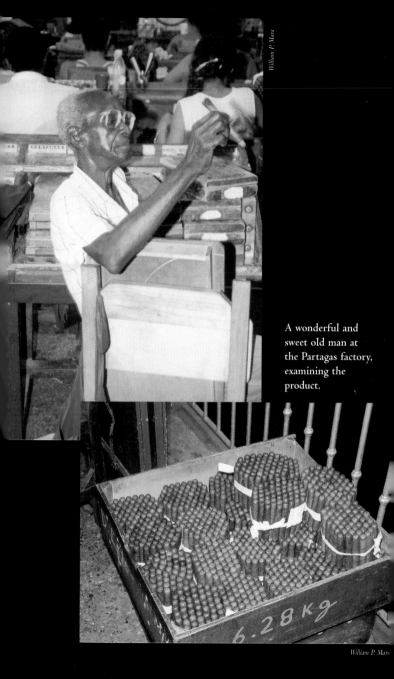

A wonderful and
sweet old man at
the Partagas factory,
examining the
product.

PARTAGAS

REAL FABRICA DE TABACOS Y CIGARROS

ESTABLECIDA   EN 1845.

A. MESS. PARTAGAS & C.

CIFUENTES Y CA.
HABANA

MADE IN HAVANA, CUBA

The famous Partagas factory in downtown Havana, established in 1845, which is open for public tours and boasts a little shop with reasonable prices.

MADE IN HAVANA, CUBA

LA FLOR DE CANO C.ª
J. CANO
· HABANA ·

SANCHO PANZA
CUESTA y Cª
HABANA

imports (as well as some of their own exports) and don't welcome the competition that would arise from the United States. Also, many businesspeople both in America and elsewhere have stated publicly that they would not even entertain the idea of trade with Cuba until Fidel Castro's rule was replaced with a democratic government. Despite reports that his health has been on the decline, many years may pass before he steps down. And it's doubtful that any of the Caribbean islands surrounding Cuba are eager to give up a portion of their American tourist market.

For now, American smokers have to satisfy themselves with cigars from other nations. Obtaining cigars from Cuba legally is possible, but the window of opportunity is a small one: You must first travel to Cuba legally, and to do that you need permission from the U.S. Treasury Department. Seventeen thousand Americans were given this permission in 1996 alone, but very few people fall into the proper categories: Professional writers and journalists may go on assignments, government representatives on official business, members of international organizations who are meeting in Cuba for bona fide reasons, and people visiting family members during a time of emergency or extreme humanitarian need. Less common are athletes, religious leaders, and academics, all of whom are reviewed by the Treasury Department on a case-by-case basis.

Americans can of course smoke Cuban cigars while visiting a foreign nation that offers habanos, but technically that too is in violation of the embargo. The point of the embargo is to keep American money out of Cuba, and any American that makes a "donation" through any route is committing a federal crime. On the other hand, it is virtually impossible for the American government to keep tabs on every United States resident who lights up a Montecristo on any visit to Canada or Germany.

One way for nonsanctioned travelers to get to Cuba is to simply go there via a third country without the Treasury Department's license. People do it all the time, sad to say. The punishment back in the States can be stiff—up to ten years in prison and/or up to $250,000 in fines—but it is rarely imposed. American travelers visiting, say, Cancún or Mexico City often cannot resist the temptation to take a day trip to Havana, where the American dollar is considered gold and everything can be bought for a reasonable price. The Cuban government is kind enough not to stamp passports but instead issues a small visa sheet, which they then throw away upon your departure. Visitors spend the day smoking great cigars and drinking smooth rum for what amounts to a pittance. Between the flight and the entertainment, a traveler might spend three hundred dollars at most, and even that is probably a high estimate. A very attractive proposal indeed.

But rather than take the risk of upsetting the U.S. government, it is safer to play by the rules and gather as much information on the embargo as possible. Such information is free for the taking from the Treasury Department's Office of Foreign Assets Control (OFAC) by phoning or faxing a request. At the time of this writing there are two OFAC locations, one in Washington, D.C., and the other in Miami. The address and phone number of the Washington division is:

> Office of Foreign Assets Control
> 1500 Pennsylvania Avenue N.W.
> Annex 2nd Floor
> Washington, D.C. 20220
> (202) 622-2500

OFAC's home page is: http://www.ustreas.gov/treasury/services/fac/fac.html.

Smuggling
and
Counterfeiting

COMBINE THE DEATHLESS MYSTIQUE OF Cuban cigars with the simple fact that they cannot be legally sold in the United States and it isn't long before two cottage industries arise: smuggling and counterfeiting.

In the case of smuggling, the United States really is the only relevant country. Other nations can give and take habanos as they please, so anyone bringing them in isn't really smuggling, per se. In the case of counterfeiting, however, the market is growing larger every day and includes not only the United States but many other nations as well. The backbone of this shadowy trade is obvious: low prices. Even the most loyal Cuban worker is aware that Cuban cigars are among the most expensive in the world. When unsuspecting consumers are offered a box of Cohiba Esplendidos for roughly one quarter the price that's being asked at the local smoke shop, chances are they're going to buy.

THE ART OF THE SMUGGLE

In the last few years, the number of Cuban cigar-smuggling incidents reported by U.S. Customs has risen by more than 200 percent. And that's based on the number of people who were *caught*. It's nearly impossible to monitor the contents of every single suitcase, wrapped parcel, and vehicle that crosses into U.S. territory. It has been estimated that the total number of Cuban cigars that make it into the mouths of American smokers each year is in the neighborhood of two to three million, although as high as ten million has been surmised. The preferred airports of cigar smugglers seem to be located on the East and West coasts: JFK in New York and the Los Angeles International Airport have notably high numbers of cigar-smuggling arrests. Of course Miami also has its fair share of incidents, probably owing to its high concentration of Cuban-Americans.

The maximum penalties for smuggling Cuban cigars, although virtually never applied, are quite harsh by anyone's standards. According to the U.S. Treasury Department's Office of Foreign Assets Control, "Penalties for violating the [Cuban embargo] sanctions range up to 10 years in prison, $1,000,000 in corporate and $250,000 in individual fines."

One of the most common ways that people get cigars into the United States is by traveling to Canada. Often they will go by train or car rather than by plane; the security blanket erected by customs officials is heaviest in airports. When traveling by car, most smokers hide their stash in some obscure place, sometimes going as far as to rig up secret storage compartments on the vehicle's underside. People traveling by train usually hide their contraband on themselves, in their socks or sleeves. Of course there always is the possibility of being frisked, but this is rare and never done without reason.

Perhaps the simplest way to smuggle Cuban cigars into the United States is by mail. Of course this usually requires having a friend in a third country who is willing to take some of the risk. In most instances the sender will remove all forms of identification (rings, boxes, and so forth) from the cigars, place them in a sturdy container, and send them on their way. The "contents" space on the mailing label is filled out fictionally, as is the name and address of the sender. This method apparently works well for the casual smoker—that is, one who isn't trying to smuggle Cuban cigars for a living and therefore doesn't mind getting only one or two boxes per year. And naturally the U.S. mail system can't possibly inspect each and every package. Still, it is just as illegal as hiding them in a car or overnight bag, and the punishment can be just as severe.

Nonprofessional smugglers figure they can buy just a box or two while abroad and bring them back without any problem. Most people of this mind simply are cigar lovers who want to experience more than just a few singles while traveling, who perhaps want to let some habanos roast in their humidors for a few weeks or months. But even this is against the law. For U.S. residents, Cuban cigars cannot be legally bought *anywhere*, and cannot be brought into the United States; *any* product of Cuban origin cannot be bought in a third country and transferred to the United States.

Many travelers tend to rationalize their positions by wondering if the customs people would really go to a lot of trouble for one or two measly boxes of cigars. Thinking this way is risky. In truth, based on past instances, very rarely are violators punished to the full extent of the law; chances are that the cigars will be confiscated and the violator sent on his or her way. *However,* it is reasonable to expect that the violator's name will be entered into a government computer somewhere, and when the person travels internationally at any other time in the future, it is likely that he or she will be searched upon return. And it will be a long, *long* time before the name is removed from this sort of blacklist.

The reason most of the small-time violators don't get the full brunt of the law rammed down their throats usually is a matter of simple practicality. The customs officials have much more important things to worry about than each and every casual cigar smoker who wants to bring home a little of the Cuban experience. Federal prosecution requires tax money, and the general public would not be too amused if millions of their tax dollars were spent trying to nail Joe Average for carrying a handful of Cohibas in a shoulder bag. And many judges agree.

Still, bringing Cuban cigars into the United States is taking a big risk. Customs officials do search through bags, and they do have trained dogs to sniff around for whatever items (usually drugs) they might not be able to find just by looking; cigars have a strong aroma, so a trained canine is going to stand a fair chance of sensing them. And the officials don't need a great deal of solid evidence to take action. Example: You're visiting a friend in Spain and you spot a box of Don Diegos for a bargain-basement price. You think, "Hey, they're not Cubans, so it must be okay to bring them back to the States." That's true, and if they're not Cuban then you're not breaking any of the embargo laws. However, if those cigars are discovered by customs agents who feel they are in fact Cuban cigars that have been disguised to look like they aren't, that's all the reason they need to relieve you of them. Infuriating, but that's how the law stands at the moment. If they suspect the cigars are Cuban and you can't *prove* otherwise, you could be in trouble.

Many lovers of Cuban cigars occasionally wonder about opportunities presented by the corrupt customs official. While it is my opinion that the large majority of customs agents are ethical, hardworking, and devout believers in what they do, there always will be exceptions. More than a few smugglers I spoke with had stories to tell of agents who only needed a modest payoff—cash, luxury items—in order to look the other way. Sometimes an official would simply want his or her share of the cigars being smuggled! Others may act as though they are interested only in doing their jobs, then will promptly take the confiscated evidence home and dispose of it "one cigar at a time." But this corruption is very much out of the ordinary.

Furthermore, the sharpened focus on cigars overall has made smuggling more difficult. Not too long ago, a smoker could stroll into the average tobacco shop in, say, New York City, and after dropping the right catch phrase or mentioning the right name, could browse through a small selection of fine Cuban smokes. Of course even then the cigars would command a premium price. But the smuggling of Cuban cigars wasn't that common and therefore not that big of a deal. Rarely were retailers caught and prosecuted, and certainly no major sting operations were in place. Nowadays no retailer in his or her right mind would take such a risk. The penalties would be too brutal: The business would be closed down, heavy fines would be issued, and people could go to jail.

The U.S. government recently carried out its first carefully planned anti–cigar smuggling effort.

It was reported not only in various national newspapers but also in the June 1997 issue of *Cigar Insider*, which reported that five people in California were arrested in April 1997 after being charged with operating an international cigar-smuggling ring. They allegedly are responsible for bringing over twenty-five thousand Cuban cigars into the United States during a period of less than one year, with business contacts not only in Cuba and the United States but also in Spain and Mexico. The arresting agents were tipped off by a businessman in Sacramento who had nearly a thousand Cuban cigars in his possession. Armed with information furnished by this man, agents were able to covertly penetrate the ring and gather evidence. When officials arrived at the home of the mastermind, they found both he and his girlfriend attempting to destroy around a hundred boxes of habanos in their fireplace.

The arrestees apparently went to Cuba on a regular basis, on commercial flights via a third country, obtaining their product from paid sources inside the Cuban cigar industry. Customers in the United States were from not only New York and California but also Idaho and Nevada, and included restaurants and nightclubs as well as individuals. Although this was the first large-scale sting operation that involved Cuban cigars, government officials expected to continue taking an aggressive role in breaking open future cases. And not only will smugglers and sellers be the focus of these future investigations, but customers as well.

Many experts believe there is a very good chance the embargo against Cuba will be lifted within the next five to ten years. If one weighs the benefits of defying the embargo with the consequences, it is obvious there is no sensible reason to take such a risk. And there are many, many fine cigars available to American smokers that are perfectly legal, some of which even come close to habanos in quality.

COUNTERFEITING

The counterfeit-cigar industry has enjoyed enormous growth over the last decade because of the increased popularity of cigars combined with the eagerness of many Cuban nationals to garner supplementary income.

If you've traveled to Cuba within the last few years and spent any time in the main cities, there's a better-than-average chance you've been approached by a dealer of counterfeit cigars. These people, mostly male, are simply everywhere, waiting to

pounce on whoever seems like a potential buyer—
that is, an unsuspecting tourist, especially one seen
smoking a cigar. To be fair, these dealers are not overly
aggressive, and when you understand their motive,
they seem less bothersome. There is no doubt that
what they're doing is illegal and a bottomless source
of irritation for their government, but most of them
simply are trying to make extra money.

The dealers will approach potential customers even in broad daylight, in the most subtle
and casual manner, because there are armed soldiers, police, and even plainclothed investigators
on nearly every street corner. A Cuban of about
twenty-five or thirty, perhaps wearing black jeans,
worn sneakers, and an untucked short-sleeved
shirt, may approach with a warm smile and say
in a quick, low voice, "You want some cigars?
Cohiba? Montecristo? I have a friend who works
at the factory." This last line often is a lie, at least
in the sense that what the dealer is implying is that
he can get cigars taken right from the factory—
that is, cigars that are authentic. Unless for some
reason you are looking to purchase counterfeit
habanos (I almost did just for the photo opportunity), it is wise to politely refuse such offers.
Ninety-nine times out of a hundred the dealer

will simply say thank you and move on to the next potential customer. At the very most, he will try one more pitch—"They're cheap" or "I can get you whatever brand you like." But ultimately these people are not pests except perhaps by virtue of the sheer number of them.

The allure of the black-market—but often counterfeit—cigar from a buyer's standpoint is easy to understand. A box of Cohiba Esplendidos costs nearly three hundred dollars at an official store but only forty or fifty dollars from a street vendor. The average price for a black-market cigar is usually less than 25 percent of the retail price, which is pretty hard to turn down. Of course, the genuine article is rarely bought off the street, which is the downside to black-market cigars. The Cohiba Esplendidos are usually low-quality cigars *dressed up* as Cohiba Esplendidos.

Interestingly (and I'm sure the Cuban government is pulling out its collective hair at this fact), many buyers of counterfeit habanos are fully aware that the product they're paying for is of inferior quality. *But* the people they plan to give them to couldn't tell a genuine habano from a fifty-cent drugstore cigar. Counterfeit Cuban cigars could be one of the world's greatest social tools. Walk into a party or a board meeting and start handing out Montecristo No. 2's and suddenly you're the star of the show. While the grateful recipients are happily puffing away, you're secretly patting yourself on the back for scoring big with your friends or colleagues after making a meager twenty- or forty-dollar investment. And who'll ever know? The Cuban government continues its crusade to convince people that buying counterfeits is foolish because the product is so poor. Meanwhile there are thousands of buyers who couldn't care less. They're just trying to maintain an image or make a statement.

It might be assumed that since the tobacco in a counterfeit habano is still Cuban, it can't be *that* bad. The fact is a counterfeit can be downright awful. The average counterfeiter doesn't go out of his or her way to secure the finest available tobacco leaves when making fakes. In fact, they are working on the standard capitalist strategy of buying raw materials at the lowest possible price and then selling them at the highest possible price to ensure the greatest possible profit. Why would they sacrifice the added expense to make sure the tobacco was of high quality? After all, how would a buyer know until after the purchase had been made? The buyer will never see the seller again, and even if he does, the seller doesn't offer refunds.

Most of the tobacco either is purchased at the farms or at the factories, and in both cases the counterfeiters get the junk, the leftovers, the waste. Sometimes it's purchased from farms in the lesser-known growing regions, where tobacco either is not usually grown or is not grown for use in the name-brand blends. Pinar del Río and Partido are not the only agrarian regions in Cuba.

Every now and then a presumed counterfeiter will in fact be selling the genuine article. Sometimes a buyer will really luck out and get a whole box, but usually they'll only get four or five cigars (although depending on the brand this too may be worth the asking price). Sometimes a street dealer really *will* have a friend who works at a factory and steals cigars. This is rare, of course, since it is a huge risk on the part of the friend: Someone caught stealing a box of cigars at a Havana factory is soon out of a job. Still, the rewards are relatively lucrative, so some take their chances.

The sellers of the genuine black-market cigars have built up a steady but not often repeat clientele, usually made up of tourists who are well-educated in Havana cigars and know what they're getting. They'll pay, for example, fifty dollars for a box of Partagas Lusitanias rather than the often-counterfeit black-market price of thirty (the international retail price is anywhere from one hundred and fifty to three hundred dollars), but they're guaranteed the genuine article.

In a similar vein, factory workers are allowed to take a certain number of cigars per day, usually one or two. Workers who don't smoke can accumulate and sell a full box's worth in less than a month. But again, it is very difficult for a buyer to know what's genuine, and also difficult for the seller to make himself credible.

For the average tourist, everything from the cigars to the boxes looks absolutely perfect; only a real expert knows the real stuff from the fake. That is, at least until one of the counterfeits is smoked. Many a visitor to Cuba, even someone with only a passing interest in cigars, has realized he's been duped after taking a few draws on what is reputed to be one of the finest cigars in the world but actually taste like dried lawn cuttings.

One way to tell true habanos from false ones is that all boxes of Cuban cigars bear the government's distinctive green-and-white seal, which is applied to the front of the box, usually at the left, and stretches a few inches over the top and bottom. Also on the bottom of the box is something called a "factory code": Each of the main factories has one, consisting of either two or three initials:

BM: Briones Montoto
EL: El Laguito
FPG: Fernando Pérez Germán
FR: Miguel Fernández Roig
HM: Heroes de Moncada
JM: José Martí
LP: Lázaro Peña
SS: Sancti Spíritus
VSC: Villa Santa Clara

If you don't see any of these codes on a box, don't buy it. New factories do open from time to time, so try to keep abreast of such things. Also try to discern which cigars are made in which factories, because sometimes a counterfeiter will commit an oversight when trying to imprint a falsified code. Romeo y Julieta cigars, for example, are made only in the Briones Montoto factory, which was formerly called Romeo y Julieta. If you're being offered a box of Petit Julietas with an "LP" code, chances are the cigars are fakes. A good and inexpensive guide that serves this purpose is *Perelman's Pocket Cyclopedia of Havana Cigars.*

Common sense regarding the quality of the product also helps. How does the design and the construction of the box seem—sloppily or well made? Do the cigars themselves seem as if they've been rolled with care? Do the colors seem relatively uniform? The Cuban cigar industry places high standards on its products, and a real cigar worker takes great pride in his or her work; nothing leaves a factory that looks poorly made. After spending a little time around true Havana cigars, you should have no problem spotting the cheap copies.

Tourists aren't the only victims of the cigar-counterfeiting industry. Restaurants, private clubs, and even overseas retailers get targeted from time to time. A diligent counterfeiter makes contacts all over the world, using the same sales pitches while trying to move a hundred boxes of fakes as when trying to sell just one. Naturally most buyers get fooled only once, but once is all the seller needs to make a killing when unloading fifty or a hundred boxes in one shot.

A box of black-market cigars may appear to be genuine because both the box and the bands are all genuine, and one would presume that the government must keep tabs on all printers, even if there are hundreds. But the counterfeit-cigar market involves a lot of cash, and it might be worthwhile for a counterfeiter to either buy some equipment outright or to convince a printer to spend a little time during the middle of the night making up a few thousand Cohiba bands or Montecristo box labels. Fake labels and bands can also be produced on a computer and printed on color printers or color copying machines. (As depleted as Cuba's economy has become since the fall of the U.S.S.R., the country still has its share of modern technology, and many Cuban residents have access to it.) Finally, labels and bands can be stolen from the factories. A street seller may in fact be correct when claiming that the box and bands are bona fide. *But that doesn't mean the cigars are.*

∽

123

The Cuban cigar industry is losing hundreds of thousands of dollars to counterfeiters every year. It's very hard to put a stop to this shadowy business; many Cuban tobacco leaders readily admit it would be nearly impossible to quell the tide completely. The only real way to stop it is to convince the consumer that the only cigars worth buying are those sold in government-approved shops.

Cuba is already planning to take this approach. Visitors to the country will be given information on where to buy genuine habanos, and warnings on where to expect counterfeiters. The counterfeit products are portrayed as worthless junk (much of it is) and not worth even the cut-rate prices. Cuban officials also are making a concerted effort to clear counterfeiters from the streets, often through the talents of plainclothed policemen. Considering how forward the average seller must be in order to keep business going, nailing them isn't particularly difficult. And Cuba does not have as liberal a judicial system as some other countries; it is debatable if *entrapment* is a word an arrested counterfeiter can use in his defense.

The penalties for counterfeiting in Cuba are becoming more and more severe. Prison sentences and heavy fines are almost guaranteed; certainly one or the other. The average counterfeiter, after being arrested, thinks twice before going back into business. Even after being released, their names are kept on file, and their lives will never be the same.

The Cuban cigar industry also plans to make their labels and ring designs a little more difficult to duplicate, very similar to efforts at curbing currency counterfeiting. But the counterfeiters usually move with the times and evolve right along with the measures designed to stop them. Technology is at many people's fingertips, and even the most complex box label can be copied to near perfection. And what cigar lover has time to inspect every inch of a box label with a magnifying glass while standing on a Havana street corner?

Still, the Cuban government somehow often knows when a visitor has chosen to make a "donation" to the black market rather than to their own coffers. As in any other competitive enterprise, they don't take kindly to customers who have been disloyal, and they have the power to deal out retribution. Regular visitors to Cuba who buy cigars off the street one too many times may find themselves unwelcome in the future. People have been told at airports to turn around and head straight back home.

The bottom line is: Anyone who wants to experience the true utopia of a Cuban cigar should spend his or her money—a bit more of it—in a bona fide shop for the real thing. Counterfeits not only are a risky investment in the legal sense, they're almost always a disappointing smoke. Regardless of their discount price, they're just not worth it.

Travelogue

I TRAVELED TO CUBA DURING THE FIRST week of July 1997 to conduct research and take photographs for this book. As a lover of fine cigars, this was truly a journey into the promised land. As an American, however, and well accustomed to the many and varied pleasantries of American life, I found myself in a perpetual state of culture shock, having traveled only sparingly during the thirty years of my life and never to a communist nation.

The idea for the trip came about simply as a solution to a financial problem. When I signed the contract with my publisher to write his book, it was understood that I would supply not only a completed manuscript but also a selection of appropriate photographs. I knew of a few places where I could get some shots of Cuba's cigar industry, but what I did not expect was for such photographs to be so damn *expensive.* Thus, an alternate plan had to be designed, and that plan turned out to be very simple, at least in concept: I would go to Cuba and take pictures myself, as I had done for other books I'd written.

The struggle, I figured, would be in getting to Cuba properly—that is, legally, which was always my intention. I remembered a friend who traveled to Cuba on a regular basis. He is a very wealthy businessman and has a lot to lose, so I knew he was going down there with the government's blessings. But how did he get the official okay, I wondered?

I called the Treasury Department and asked for some basic information on traveling to nations that normally are off-limits to U.S. citizens. The woman I spoke with, who at first I took to be a receptionist but turned out to be one of the actual department agents, asked why I wanted such information. I told her I was thinking of going to Cuba. She quickly became very discouraging, assuring me that there were very few windows of opportunity for such travel, and that the Treasury Department could, for any reason, deny a Cuban-travel license even if the applicant seemed to fit all the requirements. I told her I wanted the information anyway. The woman sighed and said it would be on my fax machine in the morning. I already had the distinct impression that I would need to exercise considerable persistence if I was going to make any headway.

The information arrived at my house via fax a few days later, and it didn't take me long to realize that as a professional writer I was one of the few who met the qualifications. So it was *possible.* Perhaps unlikely, but still possible.

Wild with excitement, I wrote a letter (there is no official application form) to the chief of licensing at the Office of Foreign Assets Control (OFAC), stating the reasons why I believed I was a qualified applicant, along with some professional information the government wanted in order to make sure that, in a phrase, I wasn't lying. I respected the process and came to greatly respect the people who enforced it; OFAC employees take their jobs quite seriously and are devoted to upholding the terms of the embargo.

OFAC is a relatively small (about 50 employees) division of the United States Treasury Department, with headquarters in Washington,

129

D.C., and a smaller satellite office in Miami. Using their own words (culled from their official Web site), the central mission of the OFAC is as follows:

> *The Office of Foreign Assets Control of the U.S. Department of the Treasury administers and enforces economic and trade sanctions against targeted foreign countries, terrorism-sponsoring organizations and international narcotics traffickers based on U.S. foreign policy and national security goals. OFAC acts under Presidential wartime and national emergency powers, as well as authority granted by specific legislation, to impose controls on transactions and freeze foreign assets under U.S. jurisdiction. Many of the sanctions are based on United Nations and other international mandates, are multilateral in scope, and involve close cooperation with allied governments.*

Requests for Cuban travel licenses are common to the OFAC—they handle about 2500 every year. Those who have family in Cuba usually can visit for humanitarian reasons, and when relations between Cuba and the United States are relatively peaceful, legitimate family members can visit pretty much anytime. Other humanitarian-type missions involving professional people of faith (priests and so forth) or physicians usually are sanctioned, as are people delivering medical supplies or food. There are other justifiable causes, including writing and reporting. But most license requests are turned down, and someone who wants to travel to Cuba just for the sake of an interesting vacation—a cigar lover, for example—basically has no chance whatsoever of getting permission. To gain the full picture on who can and can't go to Cuba, contact the OFAC and request a four-page document entitled "What You Need to Know About the U.S. Embargo," which is part of a series of free government documents concerning Cuba.

In my case, the OFAC officials wanted a great deal of information, which I was sure they would use: proof that I was indeed a professional author and had published before (they asked for copies of my published books) and that I really did have a contract with an "official" publisher, not some guy in a garage with a computer and a copying machine. They wanted to know what travel agency I'd be using, because some are authorized to arrange trips to Cuba whereas others are not: Since very few Americans travel to Cuba legally, very few agencies are needed and hence given the okay. I obviously would have to use an agency that had a government sanction.

I was told that once the application was in the system, I would be lucky to receive a response within two or three months. I wasn't surprised, knowing that OFAC is inundated at any given moment with hundreds of Cuban travel requests. Many of them were frivolous, I came to learn, but each and every one had to be addressed. So it was with considerable shock followed by tremendous pleasure that I received my license in the mail less than four weeks after applying. I don't know how or why my application was given such priority, but I wasn't about to question it.

At first I planned the trip for mid-August, hoping the brutal summer heat in Cuba would have begun to taper off by then. But in the middle of June I received a phone call from a friend who was married to a woman who had been born and raised in Cuba; she had emigrated to the States to marry my friend, and thus had gained U.S. citizenship. She fell under the qualifications of being Cuban-born and having remaining family members down there, so it was my understanding that the U.S. government more or less let her come and go as she pleased, and she traveled to Cuba every few months. (But she was not allowed to return with Cuban cigars or any other Cuban goods, because this would allow her to continually spend American money in Cuba, which of course would violate the embargo.)

Her next excursion was scheduled for the beginning of July. In spite of the heat that would be waiting for me, I knew this was a golden opportunity. She spoke English quite well and could give me lots of inside information that I would otherwise have had to learn on my own or would never have unearthed at all. She turned out to be my most valuable asset in the long run.

So it was on a Sunday morning in early July that I boarded a plane leaving Newark International and headed southwest into Mexico, to Cancún. My new friend was with me the whole time, with weighty luggage containing gifts for her relatives: There are not as many restrictions on bringing American items into Cuba as there are on bringing Cuban items to America. For the most part, Cuba really has the greatest say in what can and can't be brought into the country, and any restrictions they have apply to travelers from all nations, not just the United States. I would come to learn that Cuban officials are fairly liberal in this regard.

Even if you are given permission by the U.S. government to travel to Cuba, it's difficult to get a direct flight, even in light of the 1998 loosening of travel restrictions. From an airline's perspective, so few Americans visit Cuba that offering such a flight wouldn't make sense. But licensed American travelers can still of course go through a third country. Cancún, Mexico City, and Nassau offer regular flights to Havana that are highly affordable (mine was under two hundred dollars, round-trip).

The moment I landed in Cancún I headed for the nearest airport shop that sold cigars. I barely acknowledged that I wasn't in an English-speaking nation anymore. I went from place to place bearing an anxious expression similar to that of a little boy lost in a department store, searching for his mother. I found no specific smoke shops, but I did eventually discover cigars in both a liquor store and a newspaper stand, which had the better selection. I paused to fully absorb the beautiful sight that lay before me: boxes and boxes of Cuban cigars, all available to anyone willing to pay the asking price. A few hours earlier they had been the forbidden fruit, but now they were as common as the newspapers and the candy! Every legendary brand was represented—Cohiba, Punch, Montecristo, Romeo y Julieta—in a variety of shapes and sizes. The only bad part was I had to make a *decision.* I couldn't smoke them all at once. Which should I try first?

I settled for a Flor de Cano in a plastic tube, because it was cheap; I would be in Havana very shortly and could get all the big-name brands I wanted for much less money. Besides, I knew that a lot of the smaller, lesser-known brands could be hard to come by in Cuba (since many are produced for very specific overseas markets and are not offered domestically), and I wanted to smoke as many brands as I could, not just the big boys.

Pleased with my purchase, I hurried back to my friend, sat down, and lit up. Then I remembered my manners and inquired about the general mentality toward public smoking in Mexico. It was a relief to be in a nation that wasn't saturated with heavy anti-smoking sentiment. I've always respected people who didn't like cigar smoke (I will not, for example, smoke in a restaurant or in a crowded outdoor venue), but it still was nice to be able to lay my concerns aside for a while and simply enjoy what I was doing.

The Cano was very smooth and aromatic at the beginning—a little strong for my taste, but still very rich and full-bodied. But about halfway through it suddenly turned very bitter and harsh. I assumed the blenders purposefully engineered the cigar to taste that way, basing the flavor on market demands. But I was surprised to find a Cuban brand so early in my trip that didn't suit my preferences.

Boarding the plane was the true start of my Cuban experience. The cabin was not exactly a model of cleanliness, with torn-up carpeting, very little lighting, and no air-conditioning at all. Worst of all, everything seemed to have a light film of grime on it—tacky to the touch. I accepted that the plane had come from a nation that was experiencing a depleted economy, but still . . . some fundamental amenities could have been provided. The temperature on the plane was easily in the 120's (F°), and the heavy scent of a few dozen people perspiring in an enclosed area didn't help. The plane was late taking off, so we sat motionless for nearly an hour with sweat running down our faces and under our clothes. A woman in the seat across the aisle from me was calmly breast-feeding one of her three children, which didn't offend me but was still a bit of a jolt (I have never witnessed this on an American aircraft). And then, as if to really punctuate the situation, a fairly good-sized cockroach scuttled into the aisle, paused momentarily, then disappeared. I closed my eyes and laughed.

Evening was settling in by the time we landed at the José Martí airport. The first wave of culture shock was beginning to thin out, and I was looking forward to retrieving my bags and heading to my hotel room, where I would take a cool shower, change into something light, and slip into sleep.

No such luck. First I had to pass through immigration, which turned out to be a line of only fifteen people but took more than three hours to get through. A person in a small and brightly lit booth took passports, either stamped them or proffered little "visa sheets" (which was what all Americans received so there was no trace of their trips—when my turn finally came I told the man that I was there by permission and didn't mind the official stamp, but he shook his head and gave me a sheet anyway), then looked up names on an outdated computer system that functioned rather slowly (and was, I was told, the reason for the sluggishness of procedure). I was told later that if my name had come up, for whatever reason, as an unwelcome guest of Cuba, I would have been turned around and sent back to Mexico. I was quite relieved to find I had not been added to this blacklist.

It then took another two hours for my friend and I to get our luggage and get out into the street, mainly because there was some sort of conflict about how much weight in luggage you were allowed to carry out of the airport, and my companion had quite a bit. This, I would conclude at the end of my trip, was typical of how things moved in Cuba. Nothing happened at any great speed, at least in comparison to the way things cooked along in the American culture I'd known all my life. One official had to confer with another, who in turn would confer with someone else. Then, much to my surprise, a fee of twenty dollars had to be paid, in cash, for myself, and nearly fifty for my friend, to cover whatever small offenses our luggage caused. After all that was taken care of, we were sent on our way. All told, it took almost five hours for us to move about a hundred feet.

I suggested we hail a taxi, but it turned out that would not be necessary, because my friend's family was waiting for her with a van. I was quite surprised to find that her family consisted of nearly a dozen people. This colossal greeting, I was told, was a fairly common practice. When a relative returned home from any type of extended trip, the whole family went to the airport.

We loaded the van and headed for my friend's childhood home. My luggage was then transferred to another car, one that belonged to a family friend, a young man of perhaps twenty-eight and one of the nicest people I've ever met, who drove me to my hotel. He spoke very little English, and my Spanish wasn't much better, but we managed to exchange names and handshakes. Then he drove on silently through the darkened streets of midnight Havana, and during that twenty-minute journey my perception of nearly everything was altered forever.

The city looked as though it had been air-bombed a few days before I got there. The roads were chewed up to the point where only a military vehicle could go more than ten miles per hour without falling apart. Many of the buildings were boarded up and badly in need of paint. Every so often there would be a gap between buildings occupied only by a pile of rubble. The streetlights were depressingly dim, and the only other illumination was provided by the occasional oil-drum fire. People were draped everywhere—in folding chairs, on the edge of the sidewalk, on low cement walls, in doorways. Some of them were lying down, others were walking along in the shadows or making out with their lovers in plain view.

139

I witnessed an armed soldier performing an on-site interrogation of two teenagers. His face seemed carved from stone, and his mouth moved as rapidly as a sewing machine. As the car passed, one of the boys glanced over at me anxiously.

The hotel was co-owned and co-run by the Cuban government and a French firm. The concierge spoke fluent English, which was pleasant enough, and I was taken to my room, which had once been occupied by notorious Chicago gangster Al Capone. The price for the room was seventy dollars per night, which is a small fortune to the average Cuban. It was spartan to say the least, but I wasn't expecting great luxury. It did have an air conditioner that was in decent shape, and everything in the bathroom functioned properly. I also had a little safe and a small refrigerator.

After a quick shower I called my wife, who had been understandably apprehensive about the trip from the start. Our conversation started out with the normal stuff—how was the flight, what time did you get there, and so forth. Then my wife asked what my first impressions of the country were. I began to tell her how much sympathy I had already developed for the Cuban people in such a short time. But no sooner had I started down this conversational avenue than I was cut off by a sharp beeping sound, followed by the dial tone. I replaced the phone and called back about an hour later. My wife scolded me for not being more careful, knowing that I was in communist territory, and I agreed to make a concerted effort to do so. After that I had no more phone problems.

The next morning I headed straight for the Partagas factory, which was less than a mile from my hotel. On the way over I got my first real taste of Cuba's daytime summer heat: A close analogy would be turning on the hot water in a shower, closing all the windows, and letting the room steam up until breathing became impossible. Every day of my weeklong stay was like this. I became dehydrated so quickly that I began drinking Coca-Cola (which, I was both surprised and pleased to discover, was available everywhere) by the gallon, even though it was not much of a thirst-quencher. Beer isn't a great rehydrator either, but it's still hard to turn one down on a hot day.

I also got my first real taste of daily life in Havana while walking the mile or so to the factory. Havana is a very bright, very lively city, much like any of the major cities in the United States—plenty of people milling about, and the sounds and scents that are typical of an urban environment. Cars honked, people laughed and yelled, and there was a lot of construction going on. In spite of financial troubles, Cuba seems to be making quite an effort to improve itself. Even the Capitolio building, right across from the Partagas factory, was undergoing structural improvement.

I stood out like a sore thumb, an obvious tourist with my camera bag over my shoulder and the camera itself bouncing off my chest. I took many photographs, mostly scenics. I didn't feel comfortable photographing people because I figured they were uncomfortable with me, which I sensed in their stares and body language. They were certainly friendly enough, courteous and helpful when I was in need of directions or other such information; most people were polite, friendly, nonaggressive, relaxed, and generally quite pleasant. I discovered that most Cubans had none of the animosity toward Americans that seems so prevalent in Castro's mind; I compared the relationship between the United States and Cuba to a marriage where the spouses have the greatest love for each other but the in-laws hate one another's guts. In fact, it seemed to me that the Cuban people have a great love and respect for and intense curiosity about Americans and American life, although they are careful not to show it, just as they are reluctant to speak about their present leader. And I must confess I had the same feelings toward them. There is, in my opinion, a very strong basis for a wonderful relationship between the peoples of both nations.

Arriving at the Partagas factory felt like a religious experience. After all the articles, all the books, and all the photos, I was finally standing in front of this ageless structure, so much a part of Cuba's cigar-making history, more a museum than a functional place of business. It was well maintained and looked as though it had been painted in recent years. There were people milling about everywhere, some obvious tourists, others obvious workers.

143

I found the factory store immediately, and electricity raced through me. At the far end of the room was a little coffee bar, and on either side were display cases filled with cigar boxes. Nearly every major brand was represented, and I was surprised to find that many of the prices were indeed steep: A bundle of twenty-five Cohiba Robustos was well over two hundred dollars. This room was obviously devoted to international visitors, many of whom could afford such a luxury. Other brands, happily, were more affordable. A bunch of twenty-five small Bolivars, for example, was well under a hundred dollars.

I took a few pictures and then went to the coffee bar, where there was a small upright case that offered some single cigars, mostly Cohiba and Partagas. I bought a Cohiba Esplendido and immediately lit up. I have never before enjoyed a cigar that so embodied the ideal flavor of tobacco: rich, full, and smooth. For the next hour I did nothing but wander around this famous little store, admiring the other products and enjoying one of the most oft-noted cigars ever made.

Then I went on a walking tour of the factory (cost: five dollars). A little tour group had formed, about a dozen in all, more than half of whom were Americans, all (aside from myself) in Cuba illegally. I even met one gentleman who lived less than twenty miles from me back home, who said that many, many Americans visited Cuba illegally: He knew at least a half dozen who did it on a regular basis.

The tour was very educational. Our guide was efficient and knowledgeable, and she was accompanied by an interpreter who spoke superb English. She led us through the factory by trailing the journey of tobacco from the room where the leaves first arrive until they become finished cigars sitting in boxes. I shot over two hundred photographs, and people didn't seem to mind having their pictures taken, which is more than I can say for some in other parts of the country. One gentleman, who was responsible for making the cigar boxes, was particularly proud of his work and would only let me photograph him standing alongside his machinery.

After strolling around Havana, I went back to the hotel for my first "real" night's stay—that is, when I was settled in and wide-awake and therefore could fully appreciate the Havana nightlife. I changed and showered—an absolute necessity considering the relentless heat and humidity—then went to the hotel restaurant for a meal. There were two restaurants, actually: one very formal dining area on the top floor where the prices were surprisingly high (prime-rib dinner: thirty-five dollars American), and an open-air café on the ground floor. I chose the latter, again for the sake of economics, and ordered a chicken sandwich. Along with two cans of Coke and some sliced vegetables (carrots and string beans), I was charged seven dollars American. Fairly reasonable, I thought, and yet I couldn't help but wonder what the average Cuban citizen working six days a week to make twenty dollars American per month would've thought.

Overall, I found the food in Cuba to be quite appetizing. The selection was fairly limited, but that wasn't surprising, and the meals I had were properly prepared and served under sanitary conditions. The service too was admirable, not only in the café but everywhere: Cubans in the service sector bent over backward to please their customers—at least in my experience. I cannot remember a single unpleasant transaction.

While I was at the café I was treated to a live three-piece band: guitar, drums, and a lead vocalist who also shook the maracas. I went up to my room and fetched my tape recorder so I could capture the band for all eternity; even now they sound as crisp and as tight as they did then. Cuba is very proud of its native music, and rightly so.

I went back to my room around eight o'clock, took a second shower (necessary), and went to bed. Between the constant running around and the brutal heat, I was exhausted. I read for a while (George Orwell's *Animal Farm),* then decided to click on the television. Back home I am not a huge TV fan, but I was curious to see what Cuban television had to offer. Imagine my surprise when I found only a handful of Cuban channels, and the rest fairly familiar: WB (from New York), CBS,

CNN, and (thank God) ESPN *and* ESPN2. I fell asleep watching a replay of Major League Baseball's Home Run Competition.

I returned to the Partagas factory for some double-checking and follow-ups the next day; I wanted to make sure I hadn't missed any good photo opportunities. I spent some time visiting stores where tobacco was sold and talking to whoever had a cigar in his mouth, and also with some men selling counterfeits (Montecristos and Cohibas). They of course would not disclose their names, but they were surprisingly generous with information.

On my way back from the factory, I hailed a cab of sorts: a man on a bicycle with a single-person carriage attached to it, almost a rickshaw. The ride from the factory back to the hotel cost me a dollar American, and I felt so bad after watching the guy huff and puff in the brutal heat for a measly dollar that I never took another carriage ride during my stay. Although I never took any taxicabs either, they were easy enough to find, both government-owned and private. The latter are illegal, mainly because the government apparently does not appreciate the competition. Nevertheless, private citizens who own cars often take riders to earn extra income. I was told that riding in the privately owned vehicles is a bit cheaper than in those owned by the government. Cars could be rented at travel agencies and at the airport, but rentals are stolen relatively frequently.

Two days before I was scheduled to leave, I took a day trip to the Pinar del Río region. I rented a car, and apparently also "rented" a driver and an interpreter. The whole package was a hundred dollars, and I was amused to learn later that this was, in essence, an illegal transaction. The Cuban government has their own sanctioned interpreters, and they prefer tourists to rely on government-owned taxis for transportation. The driver and interpreter I ended up with were both "freelancers." I should've realized something was amiss when the whole deal was decided in a fairly cryptic setting (the darkened hallway of my hotel), with words being spoken in hushed tones. I had easily found the two gentlemen by word-of-mouth.

Happily, both of my employees were very efficient, and the journey was a lot of fun. It was a gorgeous day, so we had the windows down and were chatting about everything imaginable, and I got to enjoy the beautiful Cuban countryside. The sky was blue, the land was green, and the breeze was fresh and warm. My companions had many questions about America, and I in turn had many questions about Cuba. We deviated from the topic of tobacco many times, and I was surprised to find neither men were smokers, nor were many other Cuban natives. Nonsmoking Cubans, just like Americans, usually cite their health as a reason for eschewing cigars.

The Pinar region is a land of poor farmers. My interpreter instructed me to put my emotions aside concerning this and understand that they really don't know any better and therefore are not suffering half as much as I might imagine. I did my best.

It took us nearly three hours to get from Havana to the first farm. There was no tobacco growing since planting did not begin until the fall, but there were plenty of other things to see, and plenty of people with whom to speak. We met up with one of the farm managers of the region, and he was a wealth of information. He walked me through the farming process step-by-step, furnishing much more detail than I required for this book. He also told me of many minor cigar brands that I as an international traveler would never come across any-where except in the regions of Cuba that are less popular with tourists. We stopped at a smoke shop in one of the little towns, and on his advice I pur-chased a lancero-sized cigar called Veguero. I smoked it immediately and found it to be very good; perhaps not equitable to a Cohiba lancero, but certainly as pleasant as any of the lesser Cuban export brands. And the price was hard to beat: one dollar.

By the time I was ready to return to the United States, I had accumulated a rather large quantity of Cuban cigars. Despite my permission from the Treasury Department to make the trip, I knew there still were limits to what I could bring back: no more than one hundred dollars (American currency) worth of Cuban goods. I had been very careful to keep my spending within the limit; I didn't want to have to force myself to smoke eight or nine cigars in rapid succession.

I tallied the figures and found I had seventy-five dollars worth of cigars. How could I have *underspent?!* Surely I wanted to run the bill up as close to a hundred as possible.

Then I realized I had been smoking virtually nonstop. I admit that by the time I was ready to leave I didn't want to even *see* another cigar, Cuban or not. But I also knew I would feel very differently when I got home.

But time ran out, and I returned to the United States with another twenty-five dollars to spare, which in Cuba would have bought plenty of smokes: perhaps not Cohibas or Montecristos, but some of the lower-profile brands, and in respectable quantities. Example: On our way back from the Pinar region, my two-man entourage and I had stopped at a little roadside restaurant that looked like something from the set of *Gilligan's Island*. Along with food and drink, this place had a modest selection of tourist goodies such as hats, pins, and T-shirts, as well as a few cigars: a single box of Montecristos and a single box of Cohibas. Both were much less expensive than they would have been in Havana, but they were still well out of my price range. There also were six bundles of José Piedras, which I'd tried during my second night and enjoyed tremendously. There were twenty-five to a bundle, and the price made my stomach quiver: twelve dollars. I was not in tune with where I stood with my hundred-dollar limit at the time, so I didn't buy. I later realized I could've bought not one but *two* bundles of Piedras.

Getting back into the United States was not a problem at any point along the way. As I was leaving Cuba the immigration officer took the golden visa sheet from my passport and disposed of it. I asked again if he would be willing to stamp my passport because I did, after all, have permission to visit. Again my request was politely but firmly denied, I assume because the gentleman did not feel comfortable straying from procedure, which I'm sure entailed certain risks.

In Mexico everyone's bags were thoroughly searched, probably for drugs. I made no attempt to conceal the cigars, even writing them on the declaration form. When the cigars were unearthed I was asked to produce my travel license, but after I did I was sent on my way with no problems.

I arrived back in the United States in Houston, where I had a layover en route to my ultimate destination, Newark. The customs and immigration officials were courteous and efficient. They too requested a copy of my travel license and were fully aware of what I had brought with me. I made no bones about having been in Cuba despite that there really was no official record of my visit. As in Mexico, once the officials were assured of my legitimacy, they sent me on my way without detention.

After I got home I slept for nearly twelve straight hours. Then I took a shower, unpacked my bags, and had a cigar—a Cuban cigar.

Cigar-Related Terms

ALTHOUGH I HAVE MADE A CONSCIOUS effort to avoid the extensive use of cigar jargon, particularly in Spanish, throughout this book, here are a few basic terms. Since most of these words appear in other cigar-related books and magazines, this section can be used as a handy reference. To fully accommodate the person seriously interested in the cant of the cigar industry, however, one could easily compile a vocabulary collection large enough to fill a small book of its own.

ANILLO: Band that is wrapped around a cigar and identifies its brand.

BARBACOA: Drying room at a cigar factory, often used for the filler and binder leaves.

BOFETÓN: Sheet of paper that covers the top row of cigars in a box.

CAPA LEAF: Wrapper of a cigar; the outer leaf.

CAPOTE LEAF: Binder leaf of a cigar, which holds together the filler leaves and is then covered by the wrapper leaf.

CASA DE TABACO: Barn where tobacco leaves are hung during the curing process.

CENTRO LEAVES: Leaves located in the vertical mid-region of a shade-grown tobacco plant. There are three centro levels, from top to bottom *centro gordo, centro fino,* and *centro ligero.*

CHAVETA: Flat and rounded blade used by a roller to precisely cut tobacco leaves.

COROJO: Variety of tobacco grown exclusively to produce wrapper leaves.

CORONA LEAF: Leaf found at the vertical top of a shade-grown tobacco plant, usually used for binder or filler.

CRIOLLO: Variety of tobacco grown exclusively to produce filler and binder leaves.

CROMO: Lithograph that adorns the outside of a cigar box.

CUJE: Wooden pole from which tobacco leaves are hung during curing.

FÁBRICA DE TABACO: Cigar factory.

FILETEADOR: Worker who applies lithographs to cigar boxes.

FUMA: Cigar that a factory worker is allowed to take home.

GAVILLA: Bunch of tobacco leaves that have been sorted and classified.

GOMA: Odorless organic paste used by rollers to hold a finished cigar together.

HABANO: Cuban cigar.

HECHO A MANO: At least partially handmade.

LECTOR DE TABAQUERÍA: Person who reads to the workers in a cigar factory.

LIBRE DE PIE LEAF: Leaf found at the bottom row of a shade-grown tobacco plant.

LIGA: Particular blend of cigar leaves that give a brand its distinctive flavor.

LIGERO LEAF: Leaf located at the top of a sun-grown (not protected under *tapados*) tobacco plant, usually used for filler and possesses a notably strong flavor.

MADURO LEAF: "Mature," refers to a cigar leaf that has reached its maximum growth, and is particularly sweet and darkly colored.

PILÓN: Pile of cured tobacco leaves.

RECOLECTOR: Worker responsible for the harvest.

REZAGADOR: Factory worker responsible for the sorting and classifying of leaves.

SECO LEAF: Leaf located at the vertical center region of a sun-grown (not protected under *tapados*) tobacco plant, usually used for filler and possesses a moderately strong flavor.

SEMILLERO: Soil bed where cigar seeds are first planted. Shortly after germination the tiny plants are removed and replanted in a maturing farm.

TABLA: Small wooden board on which a roller rolls and cuts leaves.

TAPADO: Cloth (often cheesecloth) covering that protects growing wrapper leaves from harsh effects of direct sunlight.

TERCIO: Bale of sorted tobacco leaves, usually around eighty.

TIEMPO: Any one of the many categories in which a tobacco leaf can be placed during the sorting and grading process.

TORCEDOR: Worker responsible for rolling cigars.

TOTALMENTE HECHO A MANO: Entirely handmade.

TRIPA: Guts of a cigar, the filler.

UNO Y MEDIO LEAF: Leaf found on the second-from-the-bottom row of a shade-grown tobacco plant.

VEGA: Farm on which tobacco is grown.

VEGUERO: Tobacco farmer.

VISTA: Lithograph on the inside lid of a cigar box.

VITOLA: Generic word for a cigar style in terms of size or shape—lonsdale and culebra, for example.

VOLADO LEAF: Leaf located at the lower region of a sun-grown (not protected under *tapados*) tobacco plant, usually used for filler or binder and possesses a fairly mild (weak) flavor.

Bibliography

BOOKS

Andriote, John-Manuel, Andrew E. Falk, and B. Henry
    Pérez. *The Art of Fine Cigars*. Boston: Bullfinch Press,
    1996.

Axelrod, Dr. Herbert R. *A Guide to the Selection, Care, and
    Smoking of Fine Cigars*. Neptune City, N.J.: TFH
    Publications, 1997.

Bati, Anwer and Simon Chase. *The Cigar Companion*
    (second edition). Philadelphia: Running Press,
    1995.

Jeffers, H. Paul and Kevin Gordon. *The Good Cigar*. New
    York: Lyons and Burford, Publishers, 1996.

Jiménez, Antonio Núñez. *The Journey of the Havana Cigar*.
    Neptune City, N.J.: TFH Publications, 1996.

Marrero, Eumelio Espino. *Cuban Cigar Tobacco: Why Cuban Cigars Are the World's Best*. Neptune City, N.J.: TFH Publications, 1996.

Mesa-Lago, Carmelo (editor). *Revolutionary Change in Cuba*. Pittsburgh: University of Pittsburgh Press, 1971.

Ortiz, Fernando. *Cuban Counterpoint: Tobacco and Sugar*. New York: Vintage Books, 1970. (Originally published as *Contrapunto Cubano del Tabaco y el Azúcar* by Jesús Montero, Havana, 1940.)

Perelman, Richard B. (compiler). *Perelman's Pocket Cyclopedia of Havana Cigars*. Los Angeles: Perelman Pioneer and Company, 1996.

Resnick, Jane. *International Connoisseur's Guide to Cigars: The Art of Selecting and Smoking*. New York: Black Dog and Levanthal Publishers, 1996.

Sheahan, John. *Patterns of Development in Latin America: Poverty, Repression, and Economic Strategy*. Princeton, N.J.: Princeton University Press, 1987.

Sherman, Joel. *Nat Sherman's a Passion for Cigars*. Kansas City: Andrews and McMeel, 1996.

del Todesco, Charles. *The Havana Cigar: Cuba's Finest*. New York: Abbeville Press, 1997. (Originally published as *Havane: Cigar de Légende* in 1996 by Editions Assouline.)

Urivazo, Enzo A. Infante. *Havana Cigars (1817–1960)*. Neptune City, N.J.: TFH Publications, 1997.

Verrill, A. Hyatt. *Cuba of Today*. New York: Dodd, Mead, and Company, 1931.

MAGAZINES

Cigar Aficionado. All issues to date.

Marvin Shanken's Cigar Insider. Volume 2, Number 6 (June 1997).

Smoke. All issues to date.

Index